Discovering Ancient Prophecies

Discovering Ancient Prophecies

Hilton Sutton, Th. D.

Hilton Sutton World Ministries
Roman Forest, Texas

Discovering Ancient Prophecies
Published by:
Hilton Sutton World Ministries
P. O. Box 1259
New Caney, TX 77357
www.hilton-sutton.org
ISBN 1-879503-22-0

Cover design by: Kristin Miller

Book production by:
Double Blessing Productions
P.O. Box 52756, Tulsa, OK 74152
www.doubleblessing.com

Printed in the United States of America.

Dedication

For the believing church.
My thanks to God the Father, the Holy Spirit and our
Lord Jesus for Their supernatural help. Also, I thank
my family and staff for the help they afforded me. To
God be the glory!

Contents

Foreword

Prior to the end of World War Two, this planet was a vastly different place. Since that time mankind has begun to experience an epic race into the future. On many fronts technology is bringing about change at ever accelerating speed. Fifty to sixty years ago who could have envisioned the hour in which we live?

But this amazing era in history was written about over twenty-five hundred years ago. From the unbelievable explosion in scientific knowledge, to the incredible masses of people who enjoy mobility as never before, ours is truly the age of which the prophets of old have spoken.

In 1948 rebirth of the nation of Isreal, and the return to that ancient land of millions of the descendants of the very people who were scattered among the nations of the Earth over nineteen hundred years ago, is another in a long list of ancient prophecies being fulfilled in this hour.

Consider also the increasing prosperity of many in this hour: this too was foretold. The upheavals of nature, new deadly contagious diseases, wars of every kind and famines speading accross the planet; even man's exploits in space are recorded with the prohecies of the Scripture.

Whithin these pages is a beginner's guide to understanding the most amazingly accurate words ever recorded covering prophesied events of the past, present, and future.

Discovering Ancient Prophecies

Chapter 1
Receiving All of God's Word

Years ago I began studying prophecy for what I thought was my own personal benefit. At that time I was going through Scripture and gleaning prophecies. I was also studying the teachings of the apostle Paul because there were times when Paul had prophesied concerning the Church.

As I was reading in the fourteenth chapter of First Corinthians, the Lord caused verse 26 to become pronounced on the page.

How is it then, brethren? When you come together, each one of you has a psalm, has a teaching, has a tongue, has a revelation, has an interpretation. Let all things be done for edification.

1 Corinthians 14:26

The last statement in this Scripture verse just jumped out at me! Again, it says: **Let all things be done for edification**. Amazing! This is saying: "When a group gathers together, let all things be done for the building up, the maturity and the equipping of all present."

When believers come together in a public service, all things are to be done for edification. We should be doing this every time we gather together, whether on a Sunday or on any day or night of the

1

week. The body of believers should come together for a time of worship and thanksgiving, and to receive ministry. In such a time, we should, as the apostle Paul states, **Let all things be done for edification.**

I was delighted when I discovered this truth.

As a small child, I began learning about Jesus in a Methodist Sunday school. I was seven years old when my mother and father were born again and Holy Spirit baptized. My father was later called to the ministry. My Granddad Sutton had been wonderfully used of God as a Methodist circuit-riding preacher.

In those early days (and sometimes today) church services were not always edifying. When things are done out of divine order, they fail to edify.

As I studied 1 Corinthians 14:26, I remembered times when erroneous presentations of Bible prophecy had failed to edify. In those years when prophetic teachers would visit our church, we had difficulty getting people to attend. Why? Because their "prophetic" message was generally one of doom and gloom or over the heads of the people.

Prophetic teachers may have taught factually, but the doom-and-gloom method of delivery ruined their message. It lacked edification. Doom and gloom never edifies the hearer, as it lends itself to the spirit of fear. The apostle Paul declares in 2 Timothy 1:7, **God hath not given us the spirit of fear.**

So I determined that everything I would do with this vast subject of prophecy would be done in a way that would edify God's people.

God's people are to be built up and encouraged, so they will then go out and do business for God among the world's people. That's where God's work must be done — among the unsaved.

All the activities of God need not be carried on inside the church. That is where you are to be ministered to and edified; then you can carry on the ministry of God among the people around you — in your neighborhood, at your workplace, where you trade and do business.

According to Mark 16:15, every believer has a right to preach the Gospel of the Lord Jesus Christ. When a believer walks out the doors of a sanctuary, he should be expecting the Holy Spirit to bring people across his path. Then as he has opportunity to minister to them the goodness of God and they accept His goodness, they discover their lives being changed.

When that happens, you will be unable to keep them from the house of God. It will not matter how they grew up or what church they may attend. Once their spiritual and physical needs are being met, it will be impossible to keep them away from growing in the grace and knowledge of the Lord (2 Peter 3:18).

Since all things are to be done unto edification, that certainly would include the teaching of prophetic books of the Bible, as well as the many prophetic statements found throughout the Scriptures.

It takes *all* of God's Word — including the prophetic writings — to enable us to become the kind of people necessary to do the work that will please and glorify God.

Be Diligent

Allow me to direct your attention to some instructions given to us from God through the writings of the apostle Paul to his spiritual son, Timothy.

When God gives us instructions in His Word, I am convinced He wants us to follow through. They are not there for us to read and say, "Oh, that's good; I guess I agree with that," but then never do anything about it.

Sadly, we still have a large percentage of God's people who are giving only mental assent to the Word of God, but that's as far as it goes. They say, "Oh, I see that...that's right," but then they never walk in accordance with that Word.

As we are reading and studying the Scriptures, we sometimes see a passage and decide, "Oh, well, that's optional." No! No! No! There is nothing — absolutely nothing! — optional about God's Word. It is instructional, and we should accept and follow it.

So let's examine a simple two-verse instruction from Paul to Timothy:

Be diligent to present yourself approved to God....
2 Timothy 2:15

Many of our people have problems with diligence. They say, "Give it to me quick! Make it simple and easy. Just don't make any demands on me." But, my friend, the Lord always calls for perseverance on the part of His children, thereby putting on more of His likeness.

This verse in the old *King James Version* says, **Study to shew thyself approved unto God**. That's part of being diligent. If you are diligent, you will become a student of God's Word. You study it and learn from it.

There are many churchgoers who expect the pastors and guest preachers to be the only ones who study the Word.

Such teaching was particularly found in Roman Catholicism. For many years, until recently, parishioners were told, "Don't read the Bible; you won't understand it. Only the priests should read and study, because they are the ones who understand it."

Members of other churches act that way too. They say, "Let the preacher, the pastor, the guest speaker do all the studying. I don't have to do that. I'll hear what he has to say and just reap the benefit."

But the statement in 2 Timothy 2:15 is for the entire Body of Christ. It is saying to us, "You be diligent, be a student, so that you can present yourself approved to God."

Rightly Dividing the Word of Truth

Continuing in verse 15:

...a worker who does not need to be ashamed, rightly dividing the word of truth.

2 Timothy 2:15

It isn't likely that one who is given to diligence will ever be ashamed or lack the ability to rightly divide the Word.

I hear folks saying such things as, "I just don't understand why So-and-so was deceived and misled. I can't believe someone I thought so spiritual could be led away by false teaching and be sidetracked into strange doctrine."

Why did that happen? Simply because that person failed to be a diligent student of the Word, lacking the ability to rightly divide the Word of Truth.

Verse 16 uses a strong word, *shun:*

But shun profane and idle babblings, for they will increase to more ungodliness.

2 Timothy 2:16

5

From these verses, we have been given instruction, and it is not optional. We are told to study the Word and be diligent to show ourselves as approved workers of God who need not be ashamed.

When we do that, we avoid being embarrassed and having to say to the Lord, "Oh, my God, I've been on the wrong track. I've believed the wrong things and followed the wrong crowd. I should have stayed with Your Word."

Stay With the Book

During my lifetime I have seen strange doctrines come and go. Having been around for more than a few years, I have watched as erroneous teachings, one after another, have been offered from the pulpit. Those teachings may have seemed exciting at their onset, but I was determined to stay with the Book. When it became apparent the teachings were not solidly based in the Word, I refused to let them take root in me.

At times, people have suggested that I hear a certain Bible teacher. When I asked about that person's soundness in the Word, I was told that maybe 75 to 80 percent of his teachings were very solid.

Immediately I asked, "But what about the other 20 to 25 percent?"

They responded by telling me, "Oh, he's only off the wall with some of his teachings."

That did it for me! I will not follow teachers who have strange doctrines.

If the preacher was off the wall with that much of his teachings, I wanted absolutely nothing he taught. By already being 20 to 25 percent away from God's Word, think how far off he would be in just a few more months. For such a one, there needs to be prayer, as error begets error.

We should remain good students of God's Word, able to show His approval, rightly dividing the Word of Truth. This is vital to our studying the prophetic books and statements of God's Word. We will discuss this in more detail as we continue our study of God's prophetic words.

Chapter 2
All Scripture Is Inspired by God

L et us examine another verse of Scripture. Again, God is speaking through the apostle Paul to Timothy He makes the following statement:

All scripture is given by inspiration of God....

2 Timothy 3:16

The Amplified Bible says, **Every Scripture is God-breathed**. I like that.

This verse does not limit the inspiration of God to just the New Testament. Neither does it place divine inspiration only on one's favorite Scriptures.

It says, **All scripture is given by inspiration of God**. How much Scripture? *All* Scripture. That is a strong statement. It means *all* Scripture. That includes everything from Genesis 1:1 through Revelation 22:21. No verse in between these two is any less important than another.

All sixty-six volumes which make up the Bible are given by the inspiration of God.

I am aware that we all have our favorite verses and our favorite passages of Scripture. We have our favorite books of the Bible. We have been particularly blessed by certain portions of Scripture. I am not saying that is wrong. It is wonderful. I would not take that away from you for anything.

But I have news for you. You cannot live by your favorite verse, passage, chapter or book alone. You cannot build the spiritual life God wants for you on just a few chosen parts of Scripture.

If you are attempting to live by just a part of God's Word, it would be like eating the smallest amount of natural food and still remaining alive.

We cannot build the kind of life in Christ we need with so little Scripture. It takes *all* of God's Word to bring us into spiritual maturity. Our favorite verses, passages, chapters or books are no more inspired than the rest of God's Word. *All* Scripture has been authored and inspired by the same God.

So what is there to cause us to think the rest of God's Word would not equally bless us?

When we are blessed by certain parts of God's Word, let us not forget that the remainder of His Word is designed for our edification.

If you abide in Me, and My words abide in you, you will ask what you desire, and it shall be done for you.

John 15:7

The Old Testament Is a Foundation

It seems I have spent many years studying and teaching from the Old Testament, but I have not neglected the New Testament. All the Scriptures quoted so far in this study have come from the New Testament. But it is vital that you realize the importance of the Old Testament.

To me, the Old Testament is delightful, wonderful, thrilling and exciting. It does for my spirit man what the New Testament does, and it is the foundation on which the New Testament is built.

So, as we have read, all Scripture is given by the inspiration of God. Since the apostle Paul wrote this, I have to believe it is vitally important for you and me. It is not something we can overlook.

All Scripture Is Profitable

Let's read on in this verse:

All scripture is given by inspiration of God, and is profitable....
                                                              2 Timothy 3:16

Suppose this verse had stopped right here and nothing else had been said. If that had happened, it would have been enough. It says, **All scripture is given by inspiration of God, and is profitable.** How much Scripture is given by the inspiration of God and is profitable? *All of it!* That means from Genesis 1:1 through Revelation 22:21.

Have you ever known anyone who has gone into business for the express purpose of having an unprofitable venture?

I don't think so.

Have you ever met anyone who says, "I sure hope my life is a failure"?

Of course not!

No one ever goes into business with the thought of losing money. The purpose of going into business is to make a profit and be a success in life.

We have seen in God's Word how all Scripture is given by the inspiration of God and is profitable. Our lives are to be profitable to His glory.

Divine Instructions

Let's observe some categories in which God's Word is profitable:

11

All scripture...is profitable for doctrine, for reproof, for correction, for instruction in righteousness.

2 Timothy 3:16

It is an established fact that true doctrine can be founded on nothing less than God's Word. Doctrine that is not so founded becomes false doctrine. Therefore, the Scripture is the only source of correct, profitable doctrine.

The next category is *reproof,* which means to rebuke or censure. The most powerful source of reproof, which also provides for repentance, is the infallible Word of God. This word *reproof* also means to refute that which is in error. So it is easy for us to see the value of God's Word when it comes to the necessary act of reproof.

Correction is the third category in which the Scripture is profitable. I have observed through the years that oftentimes correction has been difficult to receive by many of God's people. Rather than admit their wrongs and make a proper change toward godliness, they run. Thus, they guard their improper attitudes, words or actions, and take them with them wherever they go. Godly correction is extremely profitable when it is accepted and acted upon.

Please notice that all Scripture is designed by God to assist us in these categories.

Note if you will the final category: **for instruction in righteousness.** This simply means instruction in right living before God and man.

In Genesis, chapter 17, God speaks to Abram, whose name He later changed to Abraham. He said to him, **Walk before me, and be thou perfect** (v.1). Another word for *perfect* is "upright."[1] Then He said, **And I will make my covenant between me and thee** (v.2).

God was saying to Abram, "You walk before Me in righteousness, and I will make a covenant between the two of us."

It is the Word of God that gives us divine instructions so that our lives are profitable to the glory of God. Only then are we able to walk in the righteousness of God.

I know we are the righteousness of God in Christ Jesus (2 Corinthians 5:21). And that's wonderful. But if you really want to know about the righteousness of God, you have to spend time in His Word.

So, what then can we conclude?

The Word of God is extremely profitable for instruction in right living — *His* righteousness.

Knowing Scripture Brings Spiritual Maturity

Verse 17 is thought provoking for it says:

That the man (or woman) of God may be complete, thoroughly equipped for every good work.

2 Timothy 3:17

Let's face it. This is a simple statement; but, as with all of God's Word, it is divinely inspired. The man or woman of God is to be complete, mature, perfect and thoroughly **furnished** (KJV) or equipped for every good work.

The word *thoroughly* strongly implies that every room in the house is to be completely furnished.

How many of God's people should be sufficiently equipped for every good work?

Answer: every single one — no exceptions! Not just those who stand in the pulpit, but all those who sit in the pews.

What is it going to take to accomplish this miracle?

13

Answer: *all* the Scripture — Genesis through Revelation.

I observe so many people today trying to do a work for God when they are only partially equipped spiritually. I want to tell them, "Go back to school." By that, I mean they should be enrolled in the "school of the Holy Spirit," where they will be studying the Word of God.

No Christian desires an unprofitable life. Nor does he wish to come to the end of his human existence only to have it said he was not successful. Success is not determined by how much one has, but by how well one used the talents and abilities God gave him.

We have discovered through the teachings of the apostle Paul that, to develop a successful and profitable life, we must have the help of the total Word of God. It is very evident from Paul's statements that God's Word is sufficient to bring us to spiritual maturity and equip us for the work set before us. The Scriptures also are clear that we, as individual Christians and collectively as the Church, must work to carry on the ministry of Jesus (John 14:12; Ephesians 4:11,12).

Good Works — Be a Fisher of Men

There is a field of souls that must be harvested. That harvest field is all around you. You cannot really follow Jesus without having an effect on the people around you. They should see Jesus in you.

Please understand that this is not Hilton speaking. Jesus said, **Follow me, and I will make you fishers of men** (Matthew 4:19). That's a guaranteed catch!

Maybe you have listened to the lies of the Devil and agreed with him when he said, "You're not a soul-winner." There are many people who say, "But that's not my ministry." If you have said that, then you are not following Jesus. It's that simple.

My friend, it is time for us to get serious about our assignment. Jesus is coming soon. It is time to cast off all the weights, get rid of all the besetting sins, and begin to run this race with the determination to win.

Jesus said, I will make you fishers of men. That does not mean you have to win somebody to Jesus every day, every week, every month. But a year should not go by without your having been a witness of Jesus to those around you. Let them see Jesus in you and hear your personal testimony.

Live a Successful Christian Life

It is wonderful when you are a part of a good church, where there is a fine fellowship of believers and an anointed pastor. The pastor has been set among you by the Lord Jesus (Ephesians 4:11). But I want you to realize that your pastor cannot do everything for you. It is not his job to do all the studying of God's Word for you. That is impossible.

If you grace the house of God with your presence only on Sunday morning, and never again until the next Sunday morning, you cannot convince me you are ready for the catching away of the Church.

In First Thessalonians, chapter 4, verses 16-18, the apostle Paul clearly describes the event of the glorious appearing of Jesus for the purpose of removing the Church, the Body of Christ, from the earth. This event we identify as "the Rapture." Paul further states that, at the time of this event, the Church will be glorious (Ephesians 5:27).

In Hebrews 10:25 he admonishes us to assemble ourselves together and do it more and more as we see the Day of the Lord approaching. How can we know that this Day is approaching? Because of the fulfillment of prophetic scriptures.

We must keep in mind that the Church is that body of born-again believers who have received Jesus as their Savior and Lord. According to the Scriptures, they continually work out their salvation with fear and trembling, and on a daily basis (Philippians 2:12).

All Christians should strive to walk daily with the Lord, so that at His appearing we can be caught up to meet Him in the air and say, as Paul did:

I have fought the good fight, I have finished the race, I have kept the faith.

Finally, there is laid up for me the crown of righteousness....
                                              2 Timothy 4:7,8

I believe every born-again child of God — whether man, woman or young person — desires to have a successful, productive Christian life to the glory of God.

What will it take for us to have that kind of spiritual life? Our hearts must be open to receive *all* of Scripture.

Do Even Greater Works Than Jesus

However, we cannot be complete men and women of God, thoroughly equipped for every good work, if we have permitted Satan to limit the amount of Scripture we study.

He is delighted when he can cause even one of God's children to be a student of the New Testament only, totally ignoring the Old Testament. He knows that person will never be complete, thoroughly equipped and furnished for all good works.

But in the writings of the apostle John, Jesus said, **He that believeth on me, the *works* that I do shall he do also; and *greater works than these shall he do*...**(John 14:12).

Jesus did not say, "The works that I do shall just a few of you do." He said, "The works that I do shall you do also, and greater works than these, because I am going to the Father."

What happened when Jesus went to the Father? The Holy Ghost came. He sent the Spirit of Truth to live and abide within us, His Church (John 14:17).

Why did the Holy Ghost come? To empower us and enable us to do the works of Jesus wherever we are (Acts 1:8).

You Are Rewarded for Your Works

In this study we are getting into some simple things from God's Word. We have learned how all Scripture is given by the inspiration of God and all Scripture will cause us to have a profitable life in Christ, instructing us in righteousness. By being able to go through the Word of God from Genesis to Revelation, you can become a complete child in God, thoroughly equipped and furnished to do His good works.

You may say, "But, Hilton, I'm not trying to get to heaven by works."

True, you don't get into heaven by your works.

We are not *saved* by works. If we could be saved through our works, everybody would brag about what they had accomplished. God's Word says we are saved by grace **through faith..., not of works, lest any-one should boast** (Ephesians 2:8,9).

But we are *rewarded* according to our works (Matthew 16:27; Revelation 22:12). We are instructed to do the works Jesus did, and even more. Don't try to see *how little* you can do for God; strive to see *how much* you can do for Him. Then you had better put yourself in a different category. You will never be content knowing you are not doing all you are capable of for the glory of God.

I want to emphasize again how everything that is taught and preached must edify you. It must build you up. It must inform and equip you. Then when you go out from church, you are ready to do business for God.

The Prophetic Books Were Inspired by God

As we have read, *all* Scripture is given by the inspiration of God and is profitable. By *all* Scripture, that includes both the Old Testament and the New Testament. Since it includes the Old Testament, then it includes all the books from Isaiah through Malachi, which are committed to prophecy.

The prophetic books of the Old Testament are just as inspired by God as any other books of the Bible. They are designed to instruct you in righteousness so that your life can be profitable. Their intent is to so build you up that you are thoroughly capable of doing the work of God.

The Word of God in the prophetic books has been grossly neglected. We have either walked around them or declared them unnecessary.

I have heard it said, "The prophetic books do not excite me. I know they are part of the Bible, but I don't need them." Such an attitude provides Satan with an opportunity to rob people of the Scriptures.

Announce to a congregation of 700 that you will be teaching the book of Revelation and observe how many of them return for that specialized teaching. Usually only fifty to sixty percent will be interested enough to come and hear. When you talk with those who do not want to attend the study, you will find that either they are afraid or have been brainwashed to believe they won't understand it anyway, so why go.

If that is how you feel about the prophetic books of the Bible, you are slamming the door on that part of God's Word and allowing Satan to succeed.

There has to be a reason why so many in the Church have neglected the study of the prophetic books, including the book of Revelation, and all the prophetic statements found in God's Word. The average Christian seems to have little interest in the prophetic Scriptures.

I wonder what the reason could be?

It is a simple one: spiritual opposition.

What kind of spirit? Satanic. It is not the Spirit of God that has kept godly people out of the prophetic books. God's Spirit is the Teacher; His Textbook is the Bible. The Opposition to teaching of the prophetic books must be satanic. (We will discuss this Opposition to prophecy in a later chapter.)

---

[1]James H. Strong. *Strong's Exhaustive Concordance*. Compact Ed. (Grand Rapids: Baker, 1992). "Hebrew and Chaldee Dictionary," p. 125. #8549.

Chapter 3
God's Words of Prophecy

Since our subject is the basics of studying Bible prophecy, we need to set a good foundation for understanding God's words of prophecy.

As I have mentioned, the average Christian does not have much understanding of the prophetic books or the masses of prophetic statements found in the Word of God. It is vitally necessary then for us to establish a solid foundation, but one that is quite simple.

You need to understand that the prophetic books and statements in the Scriptures are not complicated. They are not difficult. It is possible for you to understand them. You can handle them with as much ease as any other part of God's Word.

Prophetic Books in the Bible

Of the sixty-six books in the Bible, God has dedicated seventeen of them to the subject of prophetic events of the future.

Of those seventeen books, sixteen are found in the Old Testament: the books of Isaiah through Malachi.[1] One is in the New Testament: the book of Revelation. This book of Revelation is the greatest prophetic book of them all.

Prophetic Statements in the Bible

Now you may ask, "Are those the only places prophecy can be found in God's Word?"

No. Prophecy begins at the beginning — in the book of Genesis.

Amazing as it may seem, the Bible starts with a prophecy and ends with a prophecy. The Old Testament begins with a prophecy and ends with a prophecy; the New Testament begins with a prophecy and ends with a prophecy. Let no one convince you that the prophetic Scriptures are unimportant.

I have to believe when God gives this much coverage in His Textbook and dedicates it to one subject, that subject has to be of utmost importance.

Do you suppose God put all those prophetic books and statements in the Bible so He could say, "Look how thick My book is"? I think not. He did not use them as fillers.

God's first prophetic statement in the Bible is found in Genesis, chapter 3. God began prophesying as early as the time of Adam and Eve. (We will look at this particular verse in detail later in this book.)

As you study the Word of God, you will find that many prophetic statements are made throughout the Old Testament.

The book of Psalms is full of prophecy. It is amazing how many times the anointing of the prophet came upon the psalmist. He prophesied that which God wanted included in His Textbook, or it would not be there. Are these prophetic statements important? Absolutely!

Prophetic statements can be found throughout the New Testament as well.

We observe Jesus stepping into the office of prophet on numerous occasions. He was prophesying events of the future in all four gospels: Matthew, Mark, Luke and John. Generally Jesus prophesied events of the day in which you and I now live. He covered them magnificently, and in great detail. Are they important? I declare they are!

Then in the writings of the apostle Paul, as the anointing of the prophet came upon him, we find him prophesying with regard to the Church. The same is true of the apostle Peter.

One-Third of the Whole Bible!

As I have pointed out, there are seventeen prophetic books in the Bible. Beginning in Genesis, chapter 3, and Proceeding throughout the Scriptures, there are numerous prophetic statements.

Put all of those prophetic words together, and they make up more than one-third of the total content of the Bible. More than one-third! This says volumes about God having given so much space to the subject of biblical Prophecy

People will say, "I believe *every* word that's in the Book." Yet they know nothing about the prophetic books and statements in the Bible. They should be a little more truthful and say, "I believe *two-thirds* of what's in the Book." Why don't they believe the other one-third? Because they are not sure what it says.

Others will say, "I'm *Full* Gospel" But if they know little about the prophetic books and statements, they should change and say, "I'm *Two-thirds* Gospel."

You may think, *Hilton, you're not being fair.*

Why not cease making excuses for a lack of knowledge of His Word and become a serious student.

I am not writing this book to pat anyone on the back. The bottom line is God's Word. It is our textbook, our road map, our set of building plans. If we do not rely upon the Word, we will take shortcuts that will lead us in the wrong direction.

Until God's Word becomes the bottom line in your life, you are subject to being misled, deceived and tricked; and you may allow Satan to steal additional Word from you. Never forget the importance of the Word in relation to your faith.

So, wake up spiritually and make God's Word the foundation for your life. The day you do this, Satan will be under your feet. From then on, you can live a victorious life — a lifestyle available to *every* child of God.

Do Prophecies Confuse You?

Some years ago I was invited to attend a special assembly of ministers. In this gathering, approximately 400 ministers had come together. To attend this session, each person had to fit a certain criteria: either pastor a church in excess of 1,000, be head of a nationally recognized ministry, be a renowned author, or serve as president or vice president of a Bible college.

During the course of discussion on various topics, the subject of Bible prophecy came up. I was amazed when I heard members of the clergy rise and make comments like, "Bible prophecy simply isn't as important as the rest of God's Word," or "The prophecies of Scripture are best left alone; they will only confuse you."

These fellow ministers did not make the above statements with any intent of being contradictory or opposing the Scriptures. Evidently, they had not thought through what they had stated.

As I sat listening to the statements by men of God, I thought, *God, some of Your ministers are misinformed.*

Anyone who says the prophecies are of lesser importance than the rest of the Scripture is ignoring words we previously studied from the pen of Paul to Timothy:

All Scripture is given by inspiration of God, and is profitable for doctrine, for reproof, for correction, for instruction in righteousness,

that the man (or woman) of God may be complete, thoroughly equipped for every good work.

2 Timothy 3:16,17

This means there is not one verse, one passage, one chapter or one book in the Bible that is less inspired than the rest. (If you do not agree, I suggest you refer to chapters 1 and 2 of this book.)

We cannot afford to look on any of the Word as being of lesser importance than the rest. Such a Position would not be harmonious with the whole of Scriptural teachings.

Should one-third of the Book be set aside, no one would possess the biblical instructions necessary for one to become a mature child of God. The Holy Spirit is present to enable us to embrace all sixty-six books of the Bible.

If reading from the prophetic books and statements is truly confusing, then God lied when He said in His Word that He was not the author of confusion (1 Corinthians 14:33).

If the prophetic books and statements in the Bible seem to be confusing, it is Satan — not God — causing the confusion. When people say they are confused by the prophetic books and statements, they have to be listening more to Satan than to God.

Satan hates prophecy and he is always working against it. Let's find out why.

---

[1]Through the years, Bible scholars have always considered only sixteen of the Old Testament books to be prophetic. "Lamentations" is not included in the sixteen.

Chapter 4
Satan Hates Prophecy

The reason there has been so little interest within the Body of Christ in the prophetic books and statements is because Satan hates Bible prophecy.

He has worked overtime to keep God's people out of it. He tells Christians they will either be confused or lack understanding. He also minimizes the importance of the prophetic Scriptures to daily living. Consequently, many Christians are attempting to live without the benefit of the prophetic Word of God.

Hopefully this book, and books such as, *ABCs of Bible Prophecy*, will provide additional understanding of the prophetic books so they too will affect your spiritual life.

Think about it. I believe every born-again man, woman or young person desires to be all he or she can be to God's glory.

Since that is the case, we really need to study God's Word from Genesis 1:1 to Revelation 22:21. The time has come for Christians to put their foot down and stop allowing Satan to keep them out of any part of God's Word.

God's First Prophecy Was to Satan, the Serpent

Why is it that Satan hates prophecy? Because he was the first one to receive a prophecy from God. God had a word for him! The first prophetic statement in Scripture can be found in Genesis 3:15.

What had happened in this chapter? The Serpent had deceived Eve into eating of forbidden fruit. Then Adam went along with the deception; he entered into the act, knowing full well what he was doing.

Within this prophetic event, God corners the Serpent after he had performed an act of deception on Eve. God says to the Serpent:

"Because you have done this...I will put enmity between you and the woman, and between your seed and her Seed; He shall bruise your head, and you shall bruise His heel."
                                    Genesis 3:14,15

I want you to realize that the Serpent is Satan, the Devil.

There has been teaching in some circles that the Serpent and Satan are not the same. Anyone who teaches this does not know about Revelation 12:9, which says, **...that serpent of old, the Devil and Satan**. It clearly identifies the Serpent, the Devil and Satan as being one and the same.

Some "Bible teachers" come up with the strangest things; and, as usual, a number of saints accept their false teachings. The "teachers" who teach strange things are revealing their ignorance of Scripture. Christians who *Ooh!* and *Aah!* over false teachings are deceived.

This passage from Genesis, chapter 3, records God prophesying to Satan. It is the first prophecy in

Scripture — a major event — spoken by God Himself to none other than Satan, that old Serpent.

Satan's Fight Against Prophecy

Once the prophecy had been set forth, the beginning of its fulfillment became the next act. Satan was immediately placed on the defensive. He would have to either circumvent it or delay it as long as he could.

What did he do? He began to work against God's prophecy. As soon as he heard those prophetic Words from God, he caused trouble between the seed of the woman, Cain and Abel. Cain slew Abel. As a result, Cain was disinherited and went out from the presence of the Lord (Genesis 4:1-16).

As that occurred, the Devil probably thought, *God, go ahead and prophesy all You want. I can take care of it. I know how to handle Your prophecies. I'll fix them so that they can't come to pass.*

Though Adam and Eve disobeyed God and were thrust out of the Garden, they were not cut off from God, or separated from Him, as some teach. We discover that, shortly afterward, another son was born to them: Seth.

Seth was the seed of the woman by Adam to replace Abel (Genesis 4:25). Adam and Eve raised Seth to walk uprightly before God. And he did. They reared him in the fear and admonition of God. Satan could not work through Seth as he had through Cain.

Out of Seth came the righteous lineage, the family tree that produced men like Noah, Abraham, Isaac, Jacob and David. Eventually would come the Seed that would bruise Satan's head: His name is Jesus.

The Old Testament records a 4,000-year period from the time God prophesied to Satan until it was fulfilled. Through those years Satan was busy, constantly working at an impossible task: to cut off the seed of the woman Why? To prevent her seed from bruising his head as God had prophesied.

Had he succeeded, he would have made the prophecy of no effect, which would have given him a major weapon against God and His Word. He would have quickly declared, "God cannot keep His Word!"

But Satan miserably failed to accomplish his task. For 4,000 years God kept him in daily torment.

This reveals to us something about the Devil. He was consistent in his effort to cut off the seed of the woman, failing in every attempt. He was always looking over his shoulder to see whether the seed, who would bruise his head, had come on the scene. Through all those years he surely was constantly thinking, *Has the One Who is going to bruise my head shown up yet?* What misery!

Facing Defeat

With this brief story I wish to illustrate the mental condition that would influence Satan's every act.

How would you like to live every day of your life under the threat that someone is out to get you?

Every morning you would be thinking, *This may be the day!* Then that evening you would be wondering, *Someone is after me. Will it happen tonight while I'm asleep?* How terrifying to constantly be reminded by hearing over and over the words, *I'm going to get you!*

It would be like receiving a telephone call in the middle of the night and someone saying, "I'm going to kill you," then hanging up.

Your first thought: *This must be a crank call, or someone is playing a joke on me, or perhaps it was the wrong number.*

But an hour later your phone rings again. It is the same voice. He says, "This is not a prank; I don't have the wrong number; I'm going to kill you," and hangs up.

Later he calls again. He says, "Make no mistake, I'll be watching your every move. I'm going to kill you."

By early morning you are telephoning the police and the phone company to put a stop to this misery.

By the middle of the day the police have decided to monitor your line. Then the phone rings again and the same voice makes the identical threat.

The calls continue over a lengthy period of time.

What condition do you think your nerves would be in at the end of that period?

The police are watching your house and someone is going with you everywhere. But the caller continues his activity.

Finally you decide the best thing to do is to leave town. No sooner have you arrived at your destination than the phone rings. It's the same voice with the same threat. Evidently he knows your every move.

After a month of facing such emotional upheaval, the average person would be virtually insane.

For all those thousands of years Satan was faced with the threat of the fulfillment of God's prophecy in the Garden. He failed to cut off the seed of the woman. Can you imagine the mental state of Satan after 4,000 years of failure? This teaches us something about the Devil. He is a failure!

Prophecy Fulfilled

Throughout those 4,000 years, the plan of God continued to unfold in spite of Satan's opposition. He opposed Noah and fought against God's plan through Abraham, never fully succeeding.

Then the children of Israel went through a period in excess of 400 years in which God did not speak to them. That time was between the closing of the Old Testament and the beginning of the New Testament. During those years God did not send a prophet to speak to His people.

You can be sure Satan thought, *Aha! I've done it! I don't know how, when or where, but I must have done it. God is through with them!*

But God wasn't through. He worked miraculously with a woman named Elizabeth. She had been barren, but the angel Gabriel appeared to her husband and prophesied to him that she would conceive. And she did! She knew she was carrying a special child. His name would be called John, and he would be the forerunner of Him who was to bruise the Devil's head (Luke 1:5-25).

God then selected a special teenage girl to whom He gave favor. Her name was Mary. She was a virgin, who lived in Nazareth, and she was to be the mother of Jesus (Luke 1:26-35; 2:4-7).

When Jesus was born, what did Satan try to do? Kill the Baby Jesus, using King Herod to do it. Had he found Him, he would have killed Him, but he could not find Him (Matthew 2:1-18).

Finally, as an adult, Jesus came forth to begin His ministry. What did He accomplish during His ministry? He bruised Satan's head. Not just for a time — He bruised it permanently! Hallelujah!

It is not our responsibility to bruise Satan's head. All we have to do is maintain the bruise. And we do it through our relationship with Jesus.

Through Him, you and I live victoriously. He that is within us is greater than he that is in the world. Through Him we are more than conquerors (1 John 4:4; 5:4; Romans 8:37).

It was 4,000 years from the time God prophesied to the Devil until the time Jesus bruised his head. You may think it took a long time for that prophecy to be fulfilled. Not necessarily. God allowed the passing of many years due to the fact that His plan involving a chosen people had to run its course. However, Satan's misery would be extended, proving that God has no concern for him.

With the fulfillment of the prophecy, Satan had been defeated and, to this day, is seriously bruised. The acts of Jesus completed the prophecy His Father had given to Satan in the Garden of Eden following his deception of Eve.

So what did the Devil discover about the prophecies of the Scriptures?

They do come to pass!

No Love for the Devil

I want to make one point very clear: God has no regard for Satan or his feelings.

The only feeling God has for the Devil and his works is that of hatred. You and I should have no other feeling than hatred for Satan. God has no mercy on him and will not put up with him at all. Our attitude toward Satan should be the same as that of our heavenly Father.

We have been taught that God is love, and He is. Love is a major biblical theme. I question whether we can fathom the vastness and depth of God's love. However, His Book reveals His nature to be multi-faceted. Not only is He capable of endless love, but He can display anger, jealousy, grief, fierceness and wrath. We are abundantly blessed by not having to meet Him in His wrath.

Satan, An Absolute Failure

As we have learned, Satan is an absolute failure. If you want to fail, do things the way Satan does them. Accept his ways and, I can assure you, you will ultimately fail.

Since Jesus bruised his head, Satan has been struggling with the Church. After nearly 2,000 years, Satan remains a failure. He has been unable to sidetrack the Church.

Think about it for a moment. The Devil could not control the Church in the first century, and he has been unable to do so since. The true Church has been more powerful than Satan because the Church is very much alive and well here on the earth. Presently, the Church is gearing up as never before for the next mighty move of the Holy Spirit.

Never forget that through Jesus Christ we are overcoming conquerors and not designed by the Holy Spirit to accept defeat. (Romans 8:37; 1 John 5:4; Revelation 12:11). The Devil is still a failure. He has a 4,000-year track record, proving that point.

What can we say about Satan? He is a master failure! Attach your life to his, and you become part of his failure.

Can we say more about him? Yes! He is a champion loser. Jesus defeated him. Attach your life to Jesus, and through Him you can walk in victory over the Devil.

Chapter 5
Revelation — The Book
Satan Hates the Most

In the New Testament, there is only one book commit-ted to the subject of prophecy: the book of Revelation.

God authored all sixty-six books of the Bible. As the last book of the New Testament, Revelation is "God's Grand Finale" or His "Master Performance".

Any knowledgeable author always places his con-clusion or story climax in his last chapter. To place such information anywhere else would cause every-thing that followed to be anticlimactic.

The book of Revelation is the most satanically opposed book in the Bible. Satan hates it the most. He has used every trick he knows either to keep God's people out of this book entirely or to confuse them when they try to study it.

There has to be a reason why Satan hates the book of Revelation the way he does, and why he works overtime to keep God's people out of it.

"A Horror Story!"

Satan's most effective tool against the book of Revelation has been fear. Because many fear the book of Revelation, they never even read it.

Suppose a new convert, a person who has just been saved, says, "I think I'll study the book of

Revelation." Immediately some old saint will say, "No! Stay away from *that* book!"

Just mention the book of Revelation to some, and they will say, "That book frightens me!" To them the book of Revelation is a horror story.

If Revelation is a horror story, then we should just open our Bibles to that book, rip it out and throw it away. God would not want us having anything to do with it if it were a horror story.

But how can God's book of Revelation be a horror story that frightens us? God's Word says, through the apostle Paul to Timothy, **God hath not given us the spirit of fear** (2 Timothy 1:7). The spirit of fear is from our adversary, the devil.

You may say, "Well, if the One who has not given us the spirit of fear concludes the Bible with a horror story like Revelation, then He has lied to us!"

Is the book of Revelation truly a horror story? No! It is *not* a horror story — never has been, never will be!

How could God have closed His majestic Book with a horror story? He didn't!

"Doom and Gloom!"

Ordinarily, when we hear teaching or preaching from the book of Revelation, it sounds horrible. For many, it is a doom-and-gloom story.

As I was growing up, prophetic teachers held meetings in my home church. They came once a year and stayed two weeks!

From those teachers we learned about Bible prophecy, but at times they would shoot far over our heads so that we were unable to understand what they were talking about. Too often, the message delivered was one that produced troubling fear.

Although my home church had a good-sized congregation in those days, it was difficult to gather a crowd of Christians to hear the sermon delivered by the prophetic teacher. People were not attracted to a doom-and-gloom message. They had no desire to be frightened. There was enough to upset them without coming to church and being terrified concerning the future. Fear had taken the place of edification.

After an evening of hearing a prophetic teacher discuss the Antichrist and the mark of the Beast, many experienced great fear. Being present in such an intense service with strong overtones of fear, believers were often tormented for weeks by fear (1 John 4:18).

A message of doom and gloom lending itself to fear would not bear the anointing of the Holy Spirit. The Holy Spirit as the Schoolmaster and Overseer of the Word would not violate or cause to be taught anything contrary to the written Word (1 John 5:7).

Keep in mind while studying the prophetic books that God has not given us the spirit of fear. When a fearful and terrible event is described in the Scriptures, keep it in context. Such events are part of the future of those who have rejected Jesus as Savior.

The book of Revelation is not a horror story. However, we have been influenced to believe it is. Some teachers have taught the book of Revelation factually, but their presentation was one of fear; thus, eliminating the possibility of spiritual edification.

Satan's attempt to have us believe the book of Revelation to be a horror story has failed. Were it so, it would be contrary to the rest of the Bible.

"A Mystery Book!"

Perhaps you have heard it said that the Bible is full of contradictions. It is not! Don't believe what the

Devil says; Jesus called him a liar and said there is no truth in him (John 8:44).

Some people believe the book of Revelation is a book of hidden meanings, that it is not to be understood. Therefore, anyone's interpretation would be valid.

Were it indeed a book of hidden meanings, then God did not title it correctly. Instead of "The Revelation," He should have called it "The Mystery."

Regardless of what you may have heard, I want you to realize that the book of Revelation is not a doom-and-gloom message. It is not a book about the Tribulation period, the Antichrist, the mark of the Beast, the False prophet or the Battle of Armageddon. It is the revelation of Jesus Christ!

You exclaim, "I've never heard that before!"

Why the Book of Revelation?

When studying this book, you need to begin at the beginning and keep its opening verses in mind. They provide the source and authority for the Revelation.

The Revelation of Jesus Christ, which God gave Him to show His servants — things which must shortly take place. And He sent and signified it by His angel to His servant John,

who bore witness to the word of God, and to the testimony of Jesus Christ, to all things that he saw.

Revelation 1:1,2

Verse 1 is extremely important to the understanding of the entire book. There are three things about this first verse I wish to point out.

1) Its Theme Is Jesus.

The book begins with these words: **The Revelation of Jesus Christ.** That is the complete title of this book.

When you study the book of Revelation, you will realize that Jesus is the central theme, the major subject, of the book. You will find Him in chapter after chapter, as there are fifty-five references to Him within the twenty-two chapters.

It is important that the Tribulation, with all its events and personalities, be kept in right relationship to Jesus. One must not overshadow Jesus by placing more importance on symbols, events or other personalities, such as the Antichrist.

2) It Is Revealed to God's Servants.

Verse 1 clearly states that this prophecy is to be revealed to the servants of Jesus. Anyone who is born again of the Spirit is a servant and therefore has a Bible right to understand this book.

3) It Tells the Future.

Verse 1 tells us that the book of Revelation covers future events. For this reason we can observe Jesus in the past, present and future.

Jesus is the CEO over all the time frames covered in the book of Revelation. It covers the end of the church age, the seven years of Tribulation, the 1,000-year righteous reign of Jesus Christ and the beginning of eternity. Every major event which occurs is under the absolute management and control of angels, who are under the authority of Jesus.

A Book of Blessings

Chapter 1, verse 3, of Revelation is marvelous. It pronounces blessings on both the reader and the hearer. It says:

**Blessed is he who reads and those who hear the
words of this prophecy, and keep those things which
are written in it; for the time is near.**

Revelation 1:3

No interpretation is needed. This verse states that
the book of Revelation is to be a book of blessings. I
have never met anyone who did not want to be
blessed.

The book of Revelation is a dramatic, glorious and
thrilling book. It is dynamic, exciting and victorious.

Do Not Be Kept In Ignorance Anymore

You may say, "I thought this book to be about the
basics of Bible prophecy." It is. I want you to understand why Satan hates prophecy so much and does all
he can to keep God's people either ignorant or confused. He has reserved his greatest opposition for the
book of Revelation.

Since he was the first one to whom a prophecy
was given and discovered when God prophesies it
comes to pass, he hates Bible prophecy.

If it were possible, Satan would keep everyone
from reading and studying God's Word. Since he cannot do that, he will do his best to limit your study of
the Word.

Satan will use any possible means to keep you
from studying the Word. Do not permit him to succeed in robbing you of the blessings which come from
the Scriptures.

Remember, the prophet Hosea states, **My people
are destroyed for lack of knowledge** (Hosea 4:6).

Chapter 6
Process of Fulfillment

As you study the prophecies found in God's Word, you discover that there is a process of fulfillment which begins.

When first spoken, a prophecy enters into the process of fulfillment. At that moment the fulfillment has only begun. The process of fulfillment continues over the time allotted to that prophetic event.

Case in point: the prophesied restoration of Israel. In May of 1948 this restoration began. We know from Isaiah's prophecies that it will not be completed until the reign of Jesus here on earth.

One of the things that makes biblical prophecies so exciting is to discover the process of fulfillment.

By studying the prophetic books, you will become familiar with the prophecies that have been set forth.

When you find prophetic words which have not yet been fulfilled, you can then watch for God's Word to take action. One thing for sure: the prophecies will be fulfilled at some future date.

As you encounter Scriptures which have already begun to be fulfilled but have not reached their conclusion, you will be able to follow a day-by-day process of completion.

41

To have a firsthand observation of a prophetic event is a very exciting and thrilling experience. It will affect your spiritual life as you watch God having His way.

Like Labor Pains

Today the fulfillment of prophetic events is like labor pains. Let's examine words written by the apostle Paul to the church in Thessalonica:

> **For when they say, "Peace and safety!" then sudden destruction comes upon them, as labor pains upon a pregnant woman. And they shall not escape.**
>
> **1 Thessalonians 5:3**

Please notice I have placed emphasis upon the word *they*. This is not referring to the Church, the Body of Christ, but to other people.

The fulfillment of prophecies for this end-time period is like labor pains which have come upon the world. People will not escape the results of these prophesied labor pains.

Perhaps you know that when true labor pains begin they cannot be stopped. They can be speeded up or slowed down but not stopped. Labor pains continue until the time of birth.

Similarly, when prophetic events are in the process of fulfillment, they are like labor pains. They can be speeded up or slowed down but not stopped.

In recent times I have watched this occur on numerous occasions. God speeds up certain prophetic events and slows down others. Why? Because He has a timetable, and He always keeps everything right on time. No prophetic event can come to pass too quickly or too late.

God Is Having His Way!

I want you to become familiar with God's prophetic Word so that you can be excited about those events. It is thrilling to watch God's prophecies coming to pass throughout the world.

Quite often, front-page articles from newspapers and reports from television will allow you to say, "Aha! I can see God's prophetic Word being fulfilled!"

We are experiencing the most exciting hour ever on this planet. More prophecies of the Scriptures are being fulfilled right now than ever before in the history of the Church. There has never been a period in history when as much of the Word of God was being enacted as is today.

Because of increased prophetic activity, we live once again in "Bible days."

In the days of Jesus, marvelous prophecies were fulfilled. However, there were not nearly as many prophecies fulfilled then as there are today.

Today's prophetic events are as great as when Jesus walked the shores of Galilee — when He performed all manner of healings and miracles, and masses of people turned to Him. Yes, those were marvelously wonderful days. But there was not as much Scripture literally being fulfilled then as there is now.

In the days of the Early Church, as the Apostles were ministering in Jesus' name, there was not as much Scripture fulfilled through them as there is today.

We are living in the greatest biblical period that has ever existed in all of God's time.

I want you to realize that all the major events of today's world are telling us God's Word is truly being fulfilled.

And Jesus Is Coming Soon!

Today's major events are also telling us something else:

Jesus is coming soon!

You wonder, "How soon?"

I don't know. I know we cannot continue with the escalation of prophetic events without soon getting to the next series of prophetic events which culminates with the glorious appearing of Jesus. His appearing is for the express purpose of receiving a glorious Church unto Himself! (Ephesians 5:27, 1 Thesselonians 4:16-18).

What a majestic, thrilling, exciting, glorious day that will be!

God is at work today, and people are beginning to sense it; when so, they begin to respond. We live in a marvelous hour!

This tremendous day is the result of God taking action based upon the sixteen prophetic books of the Old Testament and many prophecies of the New Testament as well.

Prophecies Yet To Be Fulfilled

As we know, the outpouring of the Holy Spirit in the Upper Room at Jerusalem upon those 120 disciples was only the beginning of the fulfillment of Joel's prophecy. The prophecy still has not been completely fulfilled.

For more than 1,900 years, the prophecy of Joel has only been in the process of being fulfilled. It will not be completed until people from all nations are literally flowing into the kingdom of God. Notice Joel prophesied God's Spirit will be poured out upon *all* flesh. Such was not the case at the time of the upper-room experience.

It has taken almost 2,000 years for the people of our world to become aware of God's activities. Today I know of spiritual awakenings in Europe; Russia; Africa; the Orient; Southeast Asia; Australia; New Zealand; North, South and Central America. The out-pouring of the Holy Spirit is now more widespread than ever.

The prophets Isaiah and Micah proclaimed an identical prophetic event. Their statements are found in Isaiah 2:2 and Micah 4:1. Isaiah declares:

Now it shall come to pass in the latter days that the mountain of the Lord's house shall be established on the top of the mountains, and shall be exalted above the hills; and all nations shall flow to it.

Micah differs from Isaiah's statement in that he speaks of **peoples** rather than **nations** flowing into God's kingdom.

This tremendous event is to begin in the age of the Church and continue through the Tribulation into the 1,000-year reign of Jesus. Due to biblical interpretation[1], the word *mountain* is interchangeable with *kingdom*. Thus, we expect an outstanding spiritual awakening to sweep the earth, beginning prior to the Rapture.

I want you to realize there are other prophecies yet to be fulfilled.

Consider Israel, for example. Israel began as a nation in May of 1948.

Is Israel totally restored as the Scriptures describe? Not yet!

The nation of Israel occupies only a very small land area, slightly larger than Lake Superior. The present state of Israel covers approximately 10,000 square miles. This small area is considerably less than the lands given them through God's covenant with Abraham (Genesis 15:18).

As you are studying the Word and encounter a prophecy, check to see if the Scriptures give you information as to when the prophecy will begin to be fulfilled. Also, consider the historical record of that prophecy to determine whether it may have already been fulfilled.

For instance, Isaiah prophesied the coming of the Messiah. The prophecies which Isaiah set forth were not totally fulfilled at Jesus' birth or at the beginning of His ministry or at His resurrection. Of course, some prophecies were fulfilled when He was born — that's where it all began —but they were not *completely* fulfilled. Only when He returns at the end of the Tribulation to reign will this prophecy be completely fulfilled.

---

[1]For more information on "Biblical Rules of Interpretation," see Appendix at back of book.

Chapter 7
What Is a Prophet?

Today there are many self-appointed "prophets" in the land who seem always to be prophesying and predicting the future. We live in a time when many have been misled by false predictions.

People everywhere are seeking out astrologers, clairvoyants and spiritualist mediums. The world seems to be beating a path to their door.

At supermarket checkout stands, tabloid headlines often refer to these spiritualist mediums. Today in many cities of our country there are television ads providing telephone numbers which viewers call to contact a spiritualist medium for "direction" in their lives.

Concerning these "prophets," the prophet Isaiah declares there can come no good advice or counsel from such advisers. He proceeds to say that they cannot even save themselves, that their fire is not a fire to be warmed by (Isaiah 47:13,14).

It is human nature to desire to know what the future holds. The only accurate source of information regarding the future is the Word of God. There is no other!

A True Prophet

**...for prophecy never came by the will of man,
but holy men of God spoke as they were moved by
the Holy Spirit.**

2 Peter 1:21

In the Old Testament, prophets were holy men of God, especially called by God for a specific purpose. They were, in the strictest sense, God's personal mouthpiece or voice among His people.

The people recognized these prophets as God's men, and generally respected and listened to them.

Often these prophets were of rather unusual personality, not just the "run of the mill" type. They were characterized by their dedication, commitment and discipline to their godly calling; and they walked worthy of their vocation. They were not concerned with pleasing people; their desire was to guide God's people in His way and plan.

The anointing of the Holy Spirit upon the prophet was different from that of priest, judge or king. The office of the prophet was, to say the least, one of great importance.

Not only do sixteen of the thirty-nine Old Testament books bear the names of the prophets, but we find that God's prophets are prominent throughout the Old Testament. Such books as First and Second Kings, First and Second Samuel, and First and Second Chronicles are filled with the ministry of these prophets, both by deed and by word.

We must keep in mind that the prophets were responsible for bringing into existence much of the written Word identified as the Old Testament. Let us not make the foolish mistake of failing to recognize that the Old Testament is as inspired and anointed as is the New Testament. Again, I point out the words from 2 Timothy 3:16.

All Scripture is given by inspiration of God....

It is imperative that we consider Genesis through Revelation as God's Word, and not be partial to one of the two Testaments. Remember, it was the prophets of the Old Testament who introduced the Messiah and revealed His ministry to both Israel and the Gentiles.

But not all the prophets were called upon to bring God's written Word into being. For instance, there is no book of the Bible which bears the name of the prophet Nathan, but it was Nathan who dealt with David, king of Israel. As you study the Old Testament, you will discover many such men, all of whom were holy men of God, along with five women.

A Prophet's Words Are To Be Judged

Keep in mind that God, through Moses, established a very high criteria by which a prophet's words were to be judged. References to this can be found in Deuteronomy 13 and 18:20-22. Also, Jeremiah 14:15-16 and 23:9-40 speak of the prophets and their prophecies. Special attention must be paid to these godly instructions within the Old Testament.

In the New Testament we find these words regarding the purpose of the prophet in the Church today:

And He Himself gave some to be apostles, some prophets, some evangelists, and some pastors and teachers,

for the equipping of the saints for the work of ministry, for the edifying of the body of Christ.

Ephesians 4:11,12

The New Testament prophet is to participate in the growing up and maturing of the Body of Christ so that it — the Church — can do the work of the ministry.

Since the written Word is complete, New Testament prophets are never called upon to bring a new message of truth from God. In fact, a word spoken by a New Testament prophet must be judged, proven and tried (1 Corinthians 2:15; 1 John 4:1).

The written Word of God is the rule by which all New Testament prophetic utterances or exhortations must be judged. If what is spoken does not measure up to God's written Word, then God did not say it and the Holy Spirit had nothing to do with it. There can be no exceptions.

God has declared in Malachi 3:6 that He is God and He changes not. He further states in Psalm 119:89, Deuteronomy 4:2 and Revelation 22:18,19 that His Word is settled in heaven and therefore may not be changed, neither added to nor taken from.

God has, with simplicity, provided the means whereby a prophet or prophecy may be accurately judged and examined.

Difference Between Old Testament and New Testament Prophets

Such biblical truths concerning the New Testament prophet and his prophecies change considerably the office position of prophet from the Old Testament.

The Old Testament prophets were often speaking to either a rebellious king or a rebellious, backslidden congregation. Generally, their themes were repentance, correction and uprightness before God.

In His mercy God also used the Old Testament prophet to pronounce judgment and declare a future of captive enslavement or destruction for those who would not heed the Word of the Lord.

The New Testament prophet must speak so as to edify, comfort or exhort the Body of Christ, the Church (1 Corinthians 14:3). Please keep in mind that the Church today is neither rebellious nor backslidden.

True, there may be certain ones among us who have become rebellious, but they must be dealt with individually and, first of all, by their pastor.

If a rebellious Christian refuses to heed the pastor's counsel, then God can and will send one of His prophets to share His Word with that defiant one. The prophet of God coming with God's Word will assist that rebellious Christian's return to a right relationship with his pastor, his fellow saints and the Body of Christ.

The consequences are severe for any who will not hear and accept such a word through God's prophet.

Office of Prophet
vs.
Gift of Prophecy

Simply because a person may prophesy God's Word to the Body of Christ *does not* make that person a prophet or prophetess (1 Corinthians 14:31).

The use of the gift of prophecy, as set forth in chapters 12 and 14 of First Corinthians, is directed by the Holy Spirit **as He wills** (1 Corinthians 12:11).

Do not, therefore, confuse the office of the prophet with the gift of prophecy. A truly called prophet will indeed be enabled by the gift; but the gift can, and should, be occasionally used — when the Holy Spirit leads — by all believers for the spiritual benefit of others.

Chapter 8
The Old Testament Prophets and Their Prophetic Books

As previously mentioned, the Old Testament includes sixteen books written by God's prophets. Let's take a look at each of these prophetic books.

Keep in mind that the prophets were men chosen by God. It is evident they were deeply committed to their calling and spoke as the Holy Spirit directed them. They did not seek the favor of the people, but rather were concerned with the people having favor with God.

For the most part, God's Old Testament prophets were addressing a backslidden, rebellious and stiff-necked people. It certainly could not have been an easy or a delightful assignment when called upon by God to declare His coming judgments. Although the messages of God's prophets were often severe, their human personalities revealed their love for His people.

To balance the sometimes harsh predictions given through His prophets, God used them to foretell the future of Israel's restoration. These prophecies cover our time as well, which makes God's prophetic books extremely significant to the Church today.

Remember, God does not want us to be ignorant of His plan and will, so He has given us these vitally important books. If we are wise, we will not neglect the study of all sixteen of these prophetic books.

In our study, we will first share some information about each prophet, then follow with a brief analysis of the subjects covered within that prophetic book.

THE PROPHET ISAIAH

The prophet Isaiah began his ministry in the year of King Uzziah's death, about B.C. 740. His ministry and life ended when he was martyred under King Manasseh, who reigned from B.C. 696 to 642. Tradition maintains that this prophet was sawed in half as a way of execution.

Isaiah grew up in the kingdom of Judah after the nation of Israel was divided north and south. His ministry placed him in Jerusalem during the times in which Jotham, Ahaz and Hezekiah served as kings of Judah. His contemporaries were the prophets Amos, Hosea and Micah.

Isaiah witnessed the Assyrian capture of the ten northern tribes of Israel with the fall of Damascus in B.C. 732 and Samaria in B.C. 721. Both Syria and Israel then became part of the Assyrian Empire.

The ministry of Isaiah as a prophet of God was largely ignored by the kings. Against Isaiah's warnings, Ahaz of Judah set up idols within the temple in Jerusalem. Assyrian attempts to conquer Judah and Jerusalem almost succeeded during the reign of King Hezekiah, about B.C. 701.

During this time Isaiah was faithful to warn the kings and people of their impending doom, which was the result of their wickedness.

This prophet predicted the fall of Judah and Jerusalem to Babylon, which occurred in the time of

Nebuchadnezzar, king of Babylon. With Isaiah's prophecies came insight of how the people would find favor with Cyrus, king of Persia, and how he would permit their return to restore Jerusalem.

Isaiah is best known in Christian circles as the prophet who foretold the coming of a Savior, the Messiah. This glorious information is found in chapters 53 through 56. Thus, Isaiah is often referred to as the "Evangelical Prophet."

Verse-by-Verse Outline: Book of Isaiah

Volume of Rebuke and Promise 1:1-6:13

First Sermon: Rebellion Confronted
With Judgment and Grace   1:1-31

Second Sermon: Present Chastisement
for Future Glory   2:1-4:6

Third Sermon: Judgment and Exile
for the Stubborn Nation   5:1-30

Fourth Sermon: Prophet Cleansed and
Commissioned by God   6:1-13

Volume of Immanuel 7:1-12:6

First Sermon: Immanuel Rejected
by Worldly Wisdom   7:1-25

Second Sermon: Speedy Deliverance
Foreshadowing Coming Deliverer   8:1-9:7

Third Sermon: Inexorable Doom of Exile
for Proud Samaria   9:8-10:4

Fourth Sermon: False Empire Vanquished;
Glorious Empire to Come   10:5-12:6

God's Judgment — Burdens Upon Nations
13:1-23:18

Upon Babylon	13:1-14:27
Upon Philistia	14:28-32
Upon Moab	15:1-16:14
Upon Damascus and Samaria	17:1-14
Upon Ethiopia	18:1-7
Upon Egypt	9:1-20:6
Upon Babylon, Second Burden	21:1-10
Upon Edom	21:11,12
Upon Arabia	21:13-17
Upon Jerusalem	22:1-25
Upon Tyre	23:1-18

First Volume of General Judgment and Promise
24:1-27:13

First Sermon: Universal Judgment for Universal Sin	24:1-23
Second Sermon: Praise to the Lord as Deliverer, Victor, Comforter	25:1-12
Third Sermon: Song of Rejoicing in Judah's Consolation	26:1-21
Fourth Sermon: Punishment for Oppressors and Preservation for God's People	27:1-13

Volume of Woes Upon Unbelievers of Israel
28:1-33:24

First Sermon: God's Dealings With Drunkards and Scoffers in Israel	28:1-29

THE PROPHET JEREMIAH

The book bearing Jeremiah's name covers an extremely interesting period. This time frame encompasses the last forty years before the destruction of Jerusalem by the Babylonians in B.C. 586. Careful attention is paid to both the religious and political conditions of Judah.

Jeremiah's faithful secretary was Baruch. Theologians and historians agree that Baruch most likely recorded the events and the prophetic messages. The messages were, for the most part, warnings from God. During Jeremiah's ministry, the priesthood became idolatrous and some "pillow" prophets went so far as to exhort the people to pay no attention to Jeremiah.

Not all of Jeremiah's years were tragic. Josiah, king of Judah from B.C. 640 to 609, was a godly leader, who brought about both political and religious reformation. It was after his death that conditions went from bad to worse for Judah and Jerusalem. During Josiah's reign, Jeremiah had great favor; but after that, he was rejected. Judah's personal rejection of Jeremiah did not hurt nearly as much as her rejection of God. Consequently, Jeremiah became known as the "Weeping Prophet."

The book of Jeremiah is not written in chronological order; therefore, the contents of the books of Kings and Chronicles are important for the complete understanding of Jeremiah's prophecies.

Verse-by-Verse Outline: Book of Jeremiah

Jeremiah, God's Warrior 1:1-33:26

The Summons: Jeremiah's Call and Commission	1:1-19
Judah's Situation	2:1-13:27
Sickness	2:1-6:30
Folly	7:1-8:3
Blindness	8:4-9:1
Treachery	9:2-22
Idolatry	9:23-10:25
Faithlessness	11:1-12:17
Stubbornness	13:1-27
Jeremiah's Encounter	14:1-25:38
Tenderness for Judah	14:1-15:9
Bitterness Because of Judah	15:10-21
Loneliness in Judah	16:1-21

Jeremiah, God's Watchman: Hastening the Word 34:1-45:5

Word of God Fulfilled	39:1-18
Gedaliah's Governorship	40:1-41:18
Final Word in Judah	42:1-43:7
Final Word in Egypt	43:8-44:30
Jeremiah Admonishes Baruch	45:1-5

Jeremiah, God's Witness to the Nation: The Lord Omnipotent Reigneth 46:1-52:34

"The Prophet Concerning the Nations" 46:1; Egypt 46:2-28; Philistia 47:1-7; Moab 48:1-47; Ammon 49:1-6; Edom 49:7-22; Damascus 49:23-27; Kedar 49:28,29; Hazor 49:30-33; Elam 49:34-39; Babylon 50:1 — 51:64; Judah 52:1-34.

THE PROPHET EZEKIEL

The name *Ezekiel* means "God is strong."[1] The period of Ezekiel's prophecies dates between B.C. 593, when he was divinely called, and B.C. 571. His divine calling is clearly set forth in the first three chapters of the book. The prophecies or messages were delivered to his fellow exiles in Babylonian captivity.

Born in B.C. 623 of a priestly family, Ezekiel grew up in Jerusalem. He lived to observe the changing times and fortunes of the people, which included Babylonian captivity in B.C. 597.

Like the prophets before him, Ezekiel foretells the eventual destruction of Jerusalem and the temple. The first twenty-four chapters of this prophetic book develop the theme of destruction and captivity. Once news of Jerusalem's destruction in B.C. 586 reaches Babylon, Ezekiel's message changes to one of future hope. He prophesies restoration of the land of Israel and its people, the house of Israel.

Chapter 36 is one of the most amazing prophecies of all. In this chapter the prophet clearly predicts the restoration of the land tilled by its own people.

Chapter 37 continues the restoration prophecy from a different aspect and includes the miracle of the two sticks. This miracle foretells the reuniting of all the tribes of Israel once the restoration begins. Today, that restoration has begun and Israel is *one* nation, not *two*, as was the case following the death of King Solomon.

Chapters 38 and 39 describe a military attempt by the power of the north (Russia) to occupy Israel. This event has not yet been fulfilled; however, the stage is presently being set. The ensuing battle is not the Battle of Armageddon as some believe. These two battles do not occur at the same site and do not present the same opponents; neither is the outcome the same.

The remainder of Ezekiel's prophecies is of future restoration and God's unfolding plan.

Verse-by-Verse Outline: Book of Ezekiel

Israel, A Rebellious House, Will Fall 1:1-24:2 7

God Sends Ezekiel as His Spokesman
to the Rebellious House   1:1-3:27

First Series of Symbolic Actions
and Their Tragic Meaning   4:1-7:27

Vision of Israel's Doom   8:1-11:25

Idolaters in the Temple   8:1-18

Judgment Upon Jerusalem   9:1-11:25

Second Series of Symbolic Actions
and Words of Doom   12:1-14:23

THE PROPHET DANIEL

The book bearing this prophet's name has been considered by some as difficult to understand and by others as inaccurate. It is, nevertheless, supported by a vast majority of renowned scholars.

Daniel's writings cover a lifetime of experiences, dating from B.C. 605 to 530. These writings describe the divine dreams and visions which came to him.

Because of the divine insight given to Daniel, the empires of Babylon, Persia and Greece are set forth, some of which were fulfilled in Daniel's lifetime, with history recording later fulfillments.

The Roman Empire does not escape Daniel's prophetic dreams and visions. Like Isaiah, Daniel predicts the coming of the One who would change the world. In chapter 2 Daniel, interpreting the king's dream, tells of "the stone." This "stone" would come during the Roman Empire and eventually cause a godly kingdom to fill the entire earth. We know this represents the coming of Jesus Christ during the Roman Empire; He brought God's kingdom to the earth and established it.

The process for filling the earth with God's kingdom has been underway for more than 1,900 years and will be completed during the coming thousand-year reign of Jesus, the Messiah.

Daniel's life reveals how God used him to rule among his captors, having great influence with Nebuchadnezzar and Belshazzar, kings of the

Babylonian Empire, and Darius, king of the Persian Empire.

The reason for the difficulty in clearly understanding this book is found in chapter 12, verse 4, when Daniel is told to **shut up the words and seal the book, even to the time of the end.** The seal upon this book was to remain until the time of the end.

Daniel identifies this "time of the end" with four irrefutable developments:

(1) the rebirth of Israel from the Holocaust, the time of trouble greater than any previously experienced by Israel;

(2) the righteous turning many to righteousness;

(3) many running to and fro, indicating a highly mobile age; and

(4) knowledge increasing.

I offer you these facts for your consideration. Without question, we are now living in the time of the end. Therefore, Daniel's book is now open.

Verse-by-verse Outline: Book of Daniel

Miscellaneous Babylonian Experiences 1:1-6:28

Captivity and Preparation for Court Service	1:1-21
Nebuchadnezzar's Fourfold Image	2:1-49
Image of Gold: Three Friends Tested by Fire	3:1-30
Tree Vision and King's Madness	4:1-37
Handwriting on the Wall	5:1-31
Darius, Daniel and the Lions' Den	6:1-28

Visions of Four Empires and a Fifth 7:1-8:27

THE PROPHET HOSEA

Apparently Hosea began his ministry during the reign of Jeroboam II, who died in B.C. 753. Hosea's writings place him in the Northern Kingdom after Israel's division. The ministry of the prophet Amos overlapped that of Hosea.

Israel's spiritual condition is that of a backslider for whom God shows His love. The theme of God's love is revealed through this prophet's personal life. Hosea's wife leaves him and their children to become a harlot, and God sends him to restore her.

God declares His love for Israel through this loving action of Hosea. Hosea's writings show both God's judgment and His mercy.

Verse-by-Verse Outline: Book of Hosea

Hosea's Heartbreaking Home Life, Caused by
Gomer's infidelity, illustrates Israel's
Unfaithfulness
> *to God 1:1-3:5*
> *The Nation Israel, Unfaithful and Unrepentant*
> *Is Challenged by the Preacher to Come Home*
> *to the Faithful God 4:1 —14:9*

A Holy God Suffers as He Sees
Foul Sin of Israel   4:1-7:16

A Just God Must Bring
Severe Judgment   8:1-10:15

A Loving God Will Provide Restoration,
Healing, Forgiveness and
Full Salvation   11:1-14:9

THE PROPHET JOEL

Little is known concerning this prophet as he offers no specific times within his writings. It is generally accepted that he prophesied approximately B.C. 830 as the contents of this book match nations and conditions of that period.

The prophet Joel warns God's people of severe judgment and calls for repentance. It was Joel who was used by God to announce the outpouring of the Holy Spirit, reiterated by the apostle Peter in Acts, chapter 2. Joel places the greater outpouring in chronological order with the restoration of Israel. Read Joel 2:18-27.

Verse-by-Verse Outline: Book of Joel

Locust Plague and Its Removal 1:1-2:27

Plague of Locusts	1:1-20
People Urged to Repent	2:1-17
God Pities and Promises Relief	2:18-27

Future Day of the Lord 2:28-3:21

Spirit of God To Be Poured Out	2:28-32
Judgment of the Nations	3:1-17
Blessing Upon Israel After Judgment	3:18-21

THE PROPHET AMOS

The name *Amos* means "burden bearer." Amos appears as a shepherd and gardener who lives in the Judean city of Tekoa, near Bethlehem. His calling takes him into the Northern Kingdom during a time of prosperity.

The prophet Amos denounces pleasure seeking, self-indulgence, idolatry, injustice and the forsaking of God's Word. (This sounds a bit like the present day) Amos warns the people and calls on them to prepare to meet God. However, to the God-fearing, he has a message of hope. He declares that the Day of the Lord will come in which the Kingdom will be reestablished and the people can dwell safely.

Verse-by-Verse Outline: Book of Amos

Prophecies Against the Nations 1:1-2:16

Superscription and Proclamation	1:1,2
Indictment of Neighboring Nations	1:3-2:3
Indictment of Judah	2:4,5
Indictment of Israel	2:6-16

Three Discourses Against Israel 3:1 — 6:14

Declaration of Judgment	3:1-15
Depravity of Israel	4:1-13
Lamentation for Israel's Sin and Doom	5:1-6:14

Five Symbolical Visions of Israel's Condition 7:1-9:10

Devouring Locusts	7:1-3
Flaming Fire	7:4-6
The Plumb Line	7:7-9
A Priest's Interruption	7:10-17
Basket of Ripe Fruit	8:1-14
Lord at the Altar Inflicting Chastisement	9:1-10

Promises of Israel's Restoration 9:11-15

THE PROPHET OBADIAH

The name *Obadiah* simply means "servant of the Lord." This is another prophet about which little is known. His prophecy and message seem to fall into the time of Jehoram, king of Judah, and invasions of Jerusalem by the Edomites. The events occur in the ninth century B.C., making Obadiah a contemporary of the prophet Elisha.

Verse-by-Verse Outline: Book of Obadiah

Oracle of the Lord Against Edom vv. 1-4
The Awful Fulfillment vv. 5-9
Esau's Sin Against his Brother Jacob vv. 10-14

Wider Context: Day of the Lord vv. 15-18
House of Jacob to "Possess Their Possessions"
vv. 19-21

THE PROPHET JONAH

Jonah was a messenger of God to Nineveh. He was called upon to warn that city's population of coming judgment. He resisted the assignment by attempting to go to Tarshish, but God returned him to Israel's coast by a great fish.

Because of this story, unbelieving theologians wish to declare this book as fiction; however, scholars and Jesus Himself make it certain to be historical. The names and places in the book of Jonah are historical, and Jesus speaks of Jonah in Matthew 12:39-40 and Luke 11:29-30.

Eventually, Jonah obeys God and goes to Nineveh. Through his messages, the people repent and God spares them. Jonah is unhappy with the results.

Verse-by-Verse Outline: Book of Jonah
Rebellious Prophet 1:1-17

The Lord Calls, Jonah Rebels	1:1-3
The Lord Interposes a Storm	1:4-6
Sailors Intervene	1:7-16
The Lord Interposes a Big Fish	1:17

Reinstated Prophet 2:1-3:10

Jonah Prays	2:1-9
The Lord Delivers Jonah	2:10
Jonah Obeys the Call	3:1-4

THE PROPHET MICAH

This prophet, a contemporary of Isaiah, lived in the Southern Kingdom near Gath. He lived during the reigns of Jotham, Ahaz and Hezekiah. The fall of the Northern Kingdom, B.C. 721-713, came in his lifetime.

Micah warns both the Northern and Southern Kingdoms of their wickedness, due to their lack of daily holiness. He declares their doom but also preaches hope for all who put their trust in God. He also prophesies the restoration of the nation and people of Israel, as well as the thousand-year reign of the Messiah, our Lord Jesus.

Verse-by-Verse Outline: Book of Micah

The Lord's Great Lawsuit With Israel 6:1-7:20

The Lord's Plea and Indictment	6:1-16
Israel's Confession of Guilt and Complaint Before the Lord	7:1-17
Who Is Like Unto the Lord? The Final Verdict	7:18-20

THE PROPHET NAHUM

The name *Nahum* means "comfort." Nahum's ministry and prophecy can be dated with that of Jeremiah, Zephaniah and Habakkuk. Nahum speaks of both the fall of Thebes in B.C. 661 and of Nineveh in B.C. 612.

The prophet Nahum shows that God will not endlessly tolerate heartless brutality, such as that of Assyria. Once this mighty empire was struck a death-blow, Nahum calls upon his people to observe their religious feasts as Assyria would never again be a threat to Jerusalem.

Verse-by-Verse Outline: Book of Nahum

Prelude 1:1-10

Introduction	1:1
Nature of God	1:2-6
His Character in Administration of Justice	1:2,3
His Character Illustrated in Nature	1:4-6
God's Administration of Justice	1:7-10
Refuge for Faithful	1:7

THE PROPHET HABAKKUK

Habakkuk's message and prophecy occurred about the time of the fall of the Assyrian Empire and the rise of the Babylonian Empire, near the end of the seventh century B.C. His writings reveal a dialogue between God and himself, the prophet.

The prophet's concern is over the oppression of the poor by the leaders in Judah. He discusses this with God and asks when God intends to do something about it.

God reveals His plan, much to Habakkuk's lack of understanding. How could God allow a wicked, ungodly people to punish Judah?

God then reveals that the just shall live by faith and have confidence in God's actions. The prophet, understanding that God will judge the Chaldeans and Babylonians, offers the prayer of thanksgiving found in chapter 3.

Verse-by-Verse Outline: Book of Habakkuk

An Oracle From God Concerning
a Heavy Prophetic Message 1:1
Problem: God Has Not Judged Moral Depravity
of Judah 1:2-4
God's Solution: Chaldeans Will Judge Judea 1:5-11
Problem: Why Are the Wicked Used to Punish
the More Righteous? 1:12-17
God's Solution 2:1-20

Righteous Remnant To Be Preserved	2:1-5
Chaldeans' Doom Assured	2:6-19
Certainty of Retribution	2:6-8,15-17
Folly of Plundering	2:9-11
Emptiness of Tyranny	2:12-14
Vanity of Idolatry	2:18,19
Sovereign Lord Is Ruling	2:20

Prophet's Response to God's Solution 3:1-19

Prayer for God to Work as in Days of Old	3:1,2
Description of God's Revelation in the Exodus Experience	3:3-15
Confession of Complete Confidence in God	3:16-19

The Prophet Zephaniah

Zephaniah makes reference to his great-grandfather, Hezekiah, believed to be the same Hezekiah who was the king of Judah.

We can date Zephaniah's ministry to the reign of Josiah, B.C. 640-609, which places this prophet as a contemporary of Jeremiah and Nahum.

The prophet warns that Judah and Jerusalem will be invaded and Jerusalem destroyed. Scholars generally accept the Babylonian invasion, between the years B.C. 605 and 586, as a fulfillment of that prophecy.

Zephaniah's words also set forth restoration of Israel and the Lord reigning in Zion.

Verse-by-Verse Outline: Book of Zephaniah

Prophecy of God's Judgments 1:1-2:3

Ancestry and Identity of Prophet	1:1
Announcement of Certain Judgment	1:2-6
Announcement of Day of the Lord	1:7-9
Day of the Lord Is Day of Woe	1:10-13
Judgment Is Not To Be Delayed	1:14-18
Exhortation to Repentance	2:1-3

God's Judgment of Nations 2:4-3:8

Destruction of Philistia Announced	2:4-7
Moab and Ammon To Be Destroyed	2:8-11
Universality of Judgment	2:12-15
The Corrupt City, Jerusalem	3:1-8

Promised Blessings 3:9-20

Salvation and Deliverance	3:9-13
Salvation Demands Praise	3:14-20

THE PROPHET HAGGAI

Haggai, along with the prophet Zechariah, encouraged the return of the people from exile to rebuild the temple. Haggai's messages can be accurately dated to the second year of Darius the Persian, which was B.C. 520.

The Persian king, Cyrus, had issued an edict in B.C. 539 for the rebuilding of the temple. The people, becoming weary with the assignment, had turned to build their own homes when the prophet stirred them afresh to go about the rebuilding of the temple under Zerubbabel and Joshua. Zerubbabel was governor and Joshua was high priest during the rebuilding years of B.C. 520-516.

It is Haggai through whom the Lord declared, **The glory of this latter house shall be greater than of the former...** (Haggai 2:9), this "former house" being the splendid temple of Solomon. In Haggai's day, sufficient wealth and materials were not available as they had been at Solomon's time.

The prophet Haggai encourages the people with this most unusual statement. What made this temple *greater?* God used King Herod of the Roman Empire to remodel and beautify the old Zerubbabel temple. It was, therefore, a fitting place for the ministry of our Lord Jesus when He entered Jerusalem. Examining the Gospels confirms this point.

Verse-by-Verse Outline: Book of Haggai

Call to Examination 1:1-6

Opening Call to Rulers	1:1,2

THE PROPHET ZECHARIAH

The word *Zechariah* means "the Lord hath remembered." The prophet Zechariah began his ministry during the eighth month of Darius' reign in B.C. 520, shortly after Haggai's first message.

According to chapter 2, verse 4, Zechariah was a young man. No record of the length of his ministry is available, although his grandfather, the prophet Iddo, was among the returning exiles from the Persian Empire in B.C. 539.

Zechariah is a prophet among the people of Israel who are rebuilding the temple. He encourages them to be obedient to God, telling them they should pay attention to God's prophets.

In chapters 1 through 6, this prophet shares a series of eight night visions. The message is one of encouragement to the builders of Jerusalem. Within the message of the visions is the revelation that God had a long-range plan for Israel.

The prophet Zechariah deals with fasting and declares that the key to relationship with God is obedience. Fasting just to fast or legalism are of no benefit and cannot replace God's love.

It is Zechariah who establishes the coming final Kingdom, ruled by Him Who was pierced. In chapter 12, verse 10, he reveals that the people of Israel will recognize the "Pierced One." He further declares that all nations will go up to Jerusalem from year to year and worship the King of Kings (Zechariah 14:16).

Verse-by-Verse Outline: Book of Zechariah
Call to Conversion 1:1-6
Visionary Disclosure of God's Purposes 1:7-6:15

Vision One: Appearance Deceived   1:7-17

Vision Two: Destroyers Destroyed   1:18-21

Vision Three: Perfect Safety
Of Open City   2:1-13

Vision Four: Satan Silenced   3:1-10
Vision Five: Temple Rebuilt
By the Spirit Alone   4:1-14

THE PROPHET MALACHI

As with many of the prophets, the name *Malachi* has a meaning. It means "My messenger." Not much is known about Malachi except from the contents of this prophetic book. The temple and Jerusalem had been rebuilt, placing this prophecy after the time of Nehemiah, B.C. 444-432.

The spiritual condition of the people then was one of apostasy, disobedience and failure to properly handle the tithes, which are God's. God warns the people of judgment because of their attitude. As usual, He speaks through the prophet concerning the God-fearing people. There are four important chapters.

Verse-by-Verse Outline: Book of Malachi

Undeniable Love: God's Love for Israel   1:1-5

Unacceptable Sacrifices: Corrupt
Offerings by Corrupt Priests   1:6-14

Unkept Obligations: Priests'
Neglect of the Covenant   2:1-9

Untrue Husbands: Rebuke for Idolatry
and Divorce   2:10-16

Unexpected Judgment: Coming of
The Lord   2:17-3:6

Unmeasured Blessing: God's Promise
If Tithes Are Forthcoming   3:7-12

Unwarranted Assertions: Sure Meting Out
Of Justice   3:13-4:3

Unforgettable Farewell: Admonition,
Promise, Threat   4:4-6

---

[1]Meanings of names throughout this chapter are taken from the following reference Bible: *The Living Word*. Copyright © 1964. Joseph W. Cain Publisher, San Antonio, Texas 78201.

Chapter 9
Prophetic Terms

When we consider Bible prophecy, we should not only think about the seventeen books and the many prophetic statements in the Bible, but we should consider something else: that there are certain prophetic terms which are found throughout the Scriptures.

For you to fully understand the subject Bible prophecy, it is important to consider these prophetic terms.

"Last Days"

The term *last days* can be found in Old Testament as well as New Testament prophecies. The *last days* cover a particular period of time.

Occasionally I hear someone say, "It appears the last days have set in." I hear sermons preached on the last days with emphasis being placed upon what is happening now.

But, in truth, these *last days* actually began more than nineteen hundred years ago. Allow me to point out how it developed.

Joel's Prophecy

As an example, Joel predicts the future outpouring of the Holy Spirit. He says:

> **And it shall come to pass afterward that I will pour out My Spirit on all flesh.**
> **Joel 2:28**

This was an amazing prophecy. It was set forth about six hundred years before it began coming to pass.

Did Joel give us a time frame? He simply said, **And it shall come to pass afterward.** Joel's time frame is connected with the word *afterward:*

And it shall come to pass *afterward* **that I will pour out My Spirit on all flesh.**

Its Fulfillment Begins

In Acts, chapter 2, we find the initial event being recorded, which began the fulfillment of this prophecy.

The event occurred in the Upper Room in the city of Jerusalem where 120 followers of Jesus were filled with the Holy Spirit. It came fifty days after Jesus' resurrection and ten days after His ascension.

When this happened among the disciples, we see a great crowd of people surrounding them because of the spiritual phenomena. Those people were very devout Jews. They had heard how something most unusual was happening in the Upper Room. The event peaked their interest, and in amazement they came to the sight.

The Time Frame Is Set

On that day God selected the apostle Peter to address the crowd of devout Jews. They had been drawn to the site of the Upper Room where 120 were speaking with other tongues as the Spirit gave them utterance.

When Peter spoke to them, he explained what had occurred. He was quoting from Joel 2:28, but he did not use the word **afterward** which Joel had used. Peter said:

But this is what was spoken by the prophet Joel:

And it shall come to pass *in the last days*, says God,
that I will pour out of My Spirit on all flesh....

Acts 2:16,17

The prophecy of Joel has been in the process of fulfillment since that Jewish feast day of Pentecost in Jerusalem. The Upper-Room experience was only the beginning of the process. The prophecy has not been completely fulfilled, even to this day.

So what did Peter do to capture the immediate attention of the devout Jews? He said, **This is what was spoken by the prophet Joel**. When he began quoting the prophet Joel, he had their undivided attention. Why? To this day, devout Jews study the books of Moses and the prophets.

When Peter spoke of Joel's words, the Jews were listening. Reiterating Joel's prophecy, Peter makes one important change: **And it shall come to pass *in the last days***. But Joel did not use the words *in the last days* as Peter did.

When Joel prophesied the event, it was in chronological order, but he could not give a time frame. The time frame could not be given until the prophecy began to be fulfilled. The Holy Spirit revealed to Peter the time frame: the last days.

As we have previously learned, once a prophecy begins to be fulfilled, then the time frame for that prophetic event can be established. Once the Holy Spirit began to be poured out in the Upper Room, the time frame in which the prophecy was to develop had begun. Its time is the *last days*.

When Did the "Last Days" Begin?

We know from Peter's statement in Acts 2:17 that the event which occurred in the Upper Room at Jerusalem was one of those "last days" events. We also know that the ministry of Jesus took place during the last days (Hebrews 1:1,2). But we cannot be dogmatic as to exactly when the last days actually began.

Did they begin with the birth of Jesus, or was it when He was baptized in water by John and His supernatural ministry was launched? We are not sure.

Perhaps they started with His glorious resurrection, or maybe they were established with that "Upper-Room experience." Again, we are not sure.

We cannot absolutely pinpoint when the last days began.

I tend to believe this time frame which we call *the last days* was instigated by the supernatural acts of God through His only-begotten Son, Jesus Christ. Somewhere in that time those days got under way. Peter had so stated: **And it shall come to pass in *the last days*, says God, that I will pour out of My Spirit on all flesh** (Acts 2:17).

We know the "upper-room experience" was a last days event, and we have experienced nearly 2,000 years of last days.

Once in a while I hear someone say, "I think we are entering the last days." No, the truth of the matter is, we are not beginning the last days; we are rapidly running out of them!

I call on you to serve God to the fullest. Make up your mind to serve God with everything that is in you — all your heart, strength, talents, resources and ability. The time for such a commitment is now — not a week or month or year from now. Pull out the stops! Let God be God in your life!

"End Times" or "Time of the End"

Another term you will encounter as you study the book of Daniel is *time of the end*.

Now I realize that this term is often used in a heavy and profound manner.

Preachers announce, "I'm going to be speaking on the time of the end." You can tell by the tone in which it is stated that their message is going to be profound and frightening. Often a cloak-and-dagger style of doom and gloom develops during the sermon. Such material will fail to edify the hearers.

The term *time of the end* was introduced in the writings of Daniel. Once Daniel received the prophetic insight from the Holy Spirit, he was told:

Shut up the words, and seal the book until the *time of the end*....
Daniel 12:4

God permits him to tell us how to know when the time of the end has come. He describes the events identified with the time of the end by stating:

...many shall run to and fro, and knowledge shall increase.
Daniel 12:4

World War II was the breaking point that set the time of the end into the process of fulfillment. This event made demands on man's ability to produce materials for war. An explosion of technology began.

Prior to the Fall, Adam used one hundred percent of his mental ability; after the Fall, that began to decrease.

Throughout historical records, it becomes evident that succeeding generations used less and less of their brain power.

Around the time of World War II, it was said that the average human was using approximately ten percent of his brain power. The vast demands of a global war forced mankind to harness and begin to use his mind more efficiently.

The term *time of the end,* or *end time,* is not related to doom and gloom. It simply means the last days are going to be fulfilled allowing the next period of time to get underway.

A more simple definition of *end time* is: "Thank God it's Friday!"

People in the workplace look forward to Friday. Why? Because the weekend is at hand, and there will be a change in activities.

The end times brings one great era to a close so that God may usher in the next one.

The era of the Church and its great labors for the glory of God come to an end. How wonderful to discover there is no doom or gloom associated with the end time.

Knowledge Is Increasing

How are we to know the time of the end has arrived? Daniel describes this period as one in which men go to and fro on the earth and knowledge vastly increases.

Do such conditions exist today? Absolutely.

Ours is the most mobile generation mankind has known. We live in a world in which mobility has become a way of life.

Many people traveling internationally can testify to the fact that airports around the world are beehives of activity.

Not only do we live in a mobile generation, but we are experiencing an explosion of knowledge. Technology of every type is rapidly increasing. Today one can purchase a new computer. However, by the time it is installed and operating, a new and better model is on the showroom floor at a lower price!

The aviation industry is a sterling example of how fast technology is advancing. Without question, we are living in a time of increasing knowledge and mobility: the end time.

The Time of the End Is Here!

Where are we? In the time of the end.

Prophetic fulfillment reveals we are not only in the last days but the time of the end has arrived.

The primary emphasis of Daniel, chapter 12, is that those who are wise — the soulwinners — will shine like the stars in heaven (vs 3). These "wise ones" will be in great quest for God, and the knowledge of God will be increasing.

The secondary emphasis is that people will be going to and fro and technology will increase, as it is today.

More than any previous generation in church history, our generation should know more about God. Our knowledge of His Word and the operation of the Holy Spirit should be ever expanding.

The biblical prophecies concerning the end time are in the process of being fulfilled. They focus on one majestic prophetic event: the glorious appearing of Jesus to receive His Body, the Church, unto Himself.

Terms Last Days and Time of the End Cover the Tribulation

The seven years designated by Daniel in chapter 9, verses 24-27, correspond to the same period of time covered in the book of Revelation and identified by Jesus in Matthew 24 as "the Tribulation."

These seven years are an exact period of time: 84 months, or 2,520 days, divided into two equal halves of 3 1/2 years, 42 months or 1,260 days. Each month of that time is exactly 30 days in length.

"And It Shall Come To Pass"

Besides the phrases *last days* and *time of the end*, there is another prophetic term I want to consider: *And it shall come to pass.* We find these words 131 times in both Old and New Testaments.

God spoke through Joel:

And it shall come to pass **afterward that I will pour out My Spirit on all flesh....**
                                                              Joel 2:28

Whenever God says, And it shall come to pass, the words which follow that term are more sure and certain to occur than the rising and setting of the sun.

No one ever questions the rising and setting of the sun.

No one has ever asked, *Now that the sun is up, will it go down?*

Such thoughts never go through our minds.

From the time God created the sun and set it into action, it has risen and set every day.

We never think about such things because they are absolutes.

The same is true regarding God's prophetic Word. If God said it, it *will* come to pass. These days we are witnessing the action of God's Word as it comes to pass.

An elementary knowledge of Bible prophecy enables us to begin to realize how important are the fulfillments of the prophecies of Scripture. There can be no doubt that God is having His way. The Bible is literally coming to pass.

Chapter 10
What Is "the Rapture"?

The word rapture does not appear in the Scriptures. The meaning of *rapture* is "ecstasy."[1] The word *ecstasy* means "overpowering joy."[2] Both these words, *rapture* and *ecstasy*, identify an event: the catching away of the Church, the Body of Christ.

There are some biblical phrases which verify this event. Let's consider them.

First of all, Jesus said:

If I go and prepare a place for you, *I will come again and receive you to Myself;* **that where I am, there you may be also.**

John 14:3

Notice His words, **receive you to Myself**.

A second reference to "the Rapture" is found in First Thessalonians 4:16-18. It states in verse 17:

Then we who are alive and remain shall be *caught up together with them in the clouds to meet the Lord in the air.* **And thus we shall always be with the Lord.**

1 Thessalonians 4:17

A third phrase comes from chapter 5 of First Thessalonians. It says:

...that whether we wake or sleep, we should live together with Him.

1 Thessalonians 5:10

91

Notice if you will that the apostle Paul follows these words with an instruction:

Therefore comfort each other and edify one another....
          1 Thessalonians 5:11

The comfort and edification of believers is of importance to our heavenly Father. The words *comfort* and *edify* mean to encourage and build up. Since Scripture exhorts us to act in this manner toward one another, we should develop this good habit.

Interestingly enough, other statements are made by both Jesus and Paul in relation to the event referred to as "the Rapture."

"Look!"

Jesus says:

Now when these things begin to happen, look up and lift up your heads, because your redemption draws near.
          Luke 21:28

I emphasize the word **look**. The apostle Paul uses the same word *look* when writing to Titus. He says:

...*looking* for the blessed hope and glorious appearing of our great God and Savior Jesus Christ.
          Titus 2:13

By adding the suffix *-ing*, this strongly implies a watching, a continued looking.

Paul uses the word *look* again in Hebrews 9:28 (KJV) when he says:

So Christ was once offered to bear the sins of many; and *unto them that look for him shall he appear* the second time without sin unto salvation.

Notice the emphasis on these words: **unto them that *look* for him shall he appear**. This particular word *look* means to eagerly anticipate the event with joyous preparation.

If you have been around New Testament believers very long, you may have heard someone quote Luke 21:28 and add the phrase *with joy*, in this manner:

Now when these things begin to happen, look up and lift up your heads *with joy*, because your redemption draws near.

The words *with joy* are not part of the verse. But again and again this verse is quoted as though they were. Why? Because of the word *look*. There is an eager, joyous anticipation of the event.

A Joyful Hope

Jesus and Paul collaborated to tell us that this event will bring about the finishing or completing of our redemption, or salvation. The final act of redemption, or salvation, will be the glorification of the physical body.

Beloved, now we are children of God; and it has not yet been revealed what we shall be, but *we know that when He is revealed, we shall be like Him*, for we shall see Him as He is.

And everyone who has this hope in Him purifies himself, just as He is pure.
                                                    1 John 3:2,3

This Scripture reveals how we will be changed at His appearing. The apostle John speaks of the anticipation of this event of change as *hope*, just as Paul did, which we read in Titus 2:13.

This event is definitely one of joy, fulfilling the hope that the Word has placed in the believer.

So we capture all of this hope, joy and change with one word: *rapture*.

The Rapture Comes Before the Tribulation

The Old Testament gives us great truths pertaining to the pre-Tribulation catching away of the Church. In Genesis 6 the ark is a type of the Rapture; the righteous were borne above the wrath of God and then brought back to the earth. In Genesis 19 God took Lot and his family out of Sodom before He poured out His wrath upon that city.

The seven-year Tribulation is **the hour of temptation, which shall come upon all the world, to try them that dwell upon the earth** (Revelation 3:10), a time of great **wrath** (Revelation 16:1).

Read carefully First Thessalonians 5:1-11 and pay close attention to verses 9-11. The only possible way for God to pour out His wrath is, first of all, to remove the Church, the Body of Christ. Verse 9 states:

God did not appoint us to wrath, but to obtain salvation through our Lord Jesus Christ .

From the anointed pen of Daniel comes revelation. Study carefully Daniel 9:24-27. You will discover Satan using his agent, the Antichrist, to enter into a seven-year agreement with Israel, which he breaks in the middle of that period. Each of Daniel's "days" are one year in length. Daniel places the Antichrist on the scene at the beginning of the Tribulation. This is confirmed by Revelation 6:1,2, which says:

Now I saw when the Lamb opened one of the seals; and I heard one of the four living creatures saying with a voice like thunder, "Come and see."

And I looked, and behold, a white horse. He who sat on it had a bow; and a crown was given to him, and he went out conquering and to conquer.

The rider of this white horse is none other than the Antichrist. His description is that of deception.

These verses do not describe Jesus, as has been erroneously taught. Let me remind you, Jesus has crowns of inheritance, conquest and merit. He is always using the two-edged Sword, and His confession is: "I have overcome the world, and all power in heaven and earth is given unto Me"(John 16:33; Matthew 28:18).

We have no choice but to agree that the Antichrist is on the earth at the very onset of the seven years of Tribulation.

One further proof of the catching away of the Church before the Tribulation is found in Second Thessalonians, chapter 2. Verse 3 says the Antichrist, referred to as **that man of sin and the son of perdition,** must be revealed. Verse 6 declares that he (the Antichrist) will be revealed in his time. Verses 7 and 8 tell us how the Wicked One cannot be revealed until the "restrainer" has been taken out of the way.

The "restrainer" is not the Holy Spirit, but the Church. Joel 2:28-32 and Acts 2:16-21 clearly establish that once the Holy Spirit has begun His earthly ministry (which began at Pentecost) He will not conclude it until the day the sun becomes black and the moon as blood, before the coming of the great and notable Day of the Lord.

Revelation 6:12-17 makes certain that the day in which Joel's prophecy is completed is the day Jesus returns in His wrath to destroy the forces of the Antichrist at Armageddon. Zechariah 14 and Revelation 19 further confirm these truths and events.

The event described in Matthew 24:30 — **the Son of Man coming on the clouds of heaven with power and great glory** — is the same as the great and the **ter-**

rible day of the Lord (Joel 2:31), the last day of the Tribulation and beginning of the Millennium (the 1,000-year reign of Christ here on the earth).

We know this because the opening statement of Matthew 24:29 gives us a time frame for events that are about to take place:

> **Immediately after the tribulation of those days the sun will be darkened, and the moon will not give its light; the stars will fall from heaven, and the powers of the heavens will be shaken.**

The first event after the Tribulation according to this verse is the darkening of the sun and moon, and stars falling from heaven striking other planets, thus shaking the very powers of heaven.

Joel 2:31,32 and Revelation 6:12-17 corroborate to confirm these cataclysmic events occurring on **the great and the terrible day of the Lord** (Joel 2:31) **or the great day of his** (the Lamb's) **wrath** (Revelation 6:17). This is the day Jesus returns to the earth and, from the Mount of Olives, destroys in one hour the forces of the Antichrist at Armageddon (See Zechariah 14:4).

Following the shaking of the heavens, which affects the sun, moon and stars, the *entire population of the earth* (such instruments as the Hubble Space Telescope will enable men to observe these events) will observe Jesus returning in the clouds with power and great glory.

> **Then the sign of the Son of Man will appear in heaven, and then** *all the tribes of the earth* **will mourn, and they will** *see the Son of Man coming on the clouds of heaven* **with power and great glory.**
>
> **Matthew 24:30**

At this time *His elect* are gathered:

And He will send His angels with a great sound of a trumpet, and they will gather together *His elect* from the four winds, from one end of heaven to the other.

Matthew 24:31

Matthew 24:29-31 is often erroneously used to support the view that the Rapture will not occur until after the Tribulation, with the emphasis on *the elect* being only the Church.

According to this viewpoint, because the elect (meaning the Church) is being gathered, the Rapture could not have occurred before the final day of the Tribulation. However, careful research of the Scriptures reveals not one elect, but four. Matthew 24:31 describes the first time the four elects are brought together.

"The Four Elects"

The word *elect* as used in the Scripture identifies those chosen of or by God; in other words, "the chosen ones." The following Scriptures clearly establish four different ones called the "elect" or "chosen." One elect is singular, while the other three involve a race of people, a special company of people from all races and the angelic orders.

Jesus, The Elect

Isaiah 42:1-4 is certainly describing none other than:

Behold! My Servant whom I uphold, *My Elect One* in whom My soul delights! I have put My Spirit upon Him; He will bring forth justice to the Gentiles.

He will not cry out, nor raise His voice, nor cause His voice to be heard in the street.

A bruised reed He will not break, and smoking flax He will not quench; He will bring forth justice for truth.

He will not fail nor be discouraged, till He has established justice in the earth; and the coastlands shall wait for His law.

First Peter 2:6 is yet an additional reference announcing Jesus as the *Elect* of God:

Therefore it is also contained in the Scripture, "Behold, I lay in Zion a chief cornerstone, *elect*, precious, and he who believes on Him will by no means be put to shame".

Based upon these Scriptures, we can accept that *Jesus* is indeed the *Elect* of God.

Israel, The Elect

The following Scriptures show us yet a second *elect*, Israel.

Isaiah 45:4 establishes that Jacob, whose name was changed to *Israel* is also the elect (Genesis 32:27,28):

For Jacob My servant's sake, and *Israel My elect*, I have even called you by your name; I have named you, though you have not known Me.

It was from Jacob, Abraham's grandson, that the sons of Israel came and the tribes of Israel began.

Romans, chapter 11, gives additional knowledge of Israel being the elect of God. I strongly recommend a study of Romans 11:11-36 as it is a most revealing chapter. According to the statements of the apostle Paul, *Israel the elect* is not forsaken by God and replaced by the Church. It is quite evident God is not through with Israel, His elect, and keenly desires that the Church, also God's elect, have good understanding of the former, present and future relationship between Himself and Israel.

I say then, have they stumbled that they should

fall? Certainly not! But through their fall, to provoke them to jealousy, salvation has come to the Gentiles.

And they also, if they do not continue in unbelief, will be grafted in, for God is able to graft them in again.

For if you were cut out of the olive tree which is wild by nature, and were grafted contrary to nature into a cultivated olive tree, how much more will these, who are natural branches, be grafted into their own olive tree?

Concerning the gospel they are enemies for your sake, but concerning the *election* they are beloved for the sake of the fathers.

For the gifts and the calling of God are irrevocable.

For as you were once disobedient to God, yet have now obtained mercy through their disobedience, even so these also have now been disobedient, that through the mercy shown you they also may obtain mercy.

For God has committed them all to disobedience, that He might have mercy on all.

Romans 11:11,23,24,28-32

The Church, The Elect

Let's take a look at the third *elect* of God, the Church.

Speaking to the Church in Colossians, chapter 3, Paul clearly declares the *Church* to also be the *elect:*

Therefore, as *the elect of God*, holy and beloved, put on tender mercies, kindness, humility, meekness, longsuffering;

bearing with one another, and forgiving one another, if anyone has a complaint against another; even as Christ forgave you, so you also must do.

But above all these things put on love, which is the bond of perfection.

And let the peace of God rule in your hearts, to which also you were called in one body; and be thankful.

Let the word of Christ dwell in you richly in all wisdom, teaching and admonishing one another in psalms and hymns and spiritual songs, singing with grace in your hearts to the Lord.

And whatever you do in word or deed, do all in the name of the Lord Jesus, giving thanks to God the Father through Him.

Colossians 3:12-17

First Peter 1:1-3 further reveals that the *Church* is the *elect:*

Peter, an apostle of Jesus Christ, to the pilgrims of the Dispersion in Pontus, Galatia, Cappadocia, Asia, and Bithynia,

elect according to the foreknowledge of God the Father, in sanctification of the Spirit, for obedience and sprinkling of the blood of Jesus Christ:

Grace to you and peace be multiplied.

Keep in mind that for the first ten years of the Church's existence, it was a Jewish body of believers. So God used His original chosen, or elect, people — the Jews — to bring into existence the Church, which eventually became basically Gentile and also became His *elect.*

In the first letter to the Church in Thessalonica, Paul writes this:

Paul, Silvanus, and Timothy, to the church of the Thessalonians in God the Father and the Lord Jesus Christ: Grace to you and peace from God our Father and the Lord Jesus Christ.

We give thanks to God always for you all, making mention of you in our prayers,

remembering without ceasing your work of faith, labor of love, and patience of hope in our Lord Jesus Christ in the sight of our God and Father,

knowing, beloved brethren, your *election* by God.

Thessalonians 1:1-4

Notice the simplicity of verse 4 and the Church's *election* by God.

Peter's final statement in First Peter 5:12-14 strengthens the Church's position as God's *elect:*

By Silvanus, our faithful brother as I consider him, I have written to you briefly, exhorting and testifying that this is the true grace of God in which you stand.

She who is in Babylon, *elect together with you*, greets you; and so does Mark my son.

Greet one another with a kiss of love. Peace to you all who are in Christ Jesus. Amen.

Angels, The Elect

Elect number four is found in First Timothy 5:21:

I charge you before God and the Lord Jesus Christ and the *elect* angels that you observe these things without prejudice, doing nothing with partiality.

What then can we conclude? *Angels* are also the *elect* of God.

Much is written within the Scriptures concerning *election.* I strongly urge you to study the truths of election to better understand your election and how to maintain it.

A Fifth Elect

As we have seen, soundly established within God's Word is the existence of *four elects* of God. As your study of the Word continues and your awareness of the election increases, you will also discover what seems to be a *fifth* elect, or chosen, of God. This chosen, or elect, group consists of His called ministers.

Acts 9:10-19 bears out this truth; Paul knew he was chosen, or elected, by God.

Luke 6:12-16 reveals Jesus choosing His disciples.

Because ministers are a fixed part of the Church, they fall into the category of the elect of the Church from which God chooses those who will become His ministers of the Word to His people.

Regarding the four elects, closely examine Matthew 24:31:

And He [Jesus, the Elect] **will send His angels** [also the elect] **with a great sound of a trumpet....**

Read Revelation 11:15-19 to discover this is the trumpet sounded by the seventh angel on the last day of the Tribulation. Do not confuse this trumpet with the trumpet of God in 1 Corinthians 15:51-53 and 1 Thessalonians 4:16-18.

"The Four Winds"

Matthew 24:31 continues:

...and they (the elect angels) **will gather together** *His elect* **from the** *four winds*, **from one end of heaven to the other.**

Throughout the Bible, the reference *four winds* identifies the earth. So the *elect angels* will gather the *elect* of God from all over the earth. Who are they? Revelation 12:13-17 reveals a remnant of Israel hidden from the Antichrist for the last forty-two months of the

Tribulation. Remember, Israel is also one of the *elects* and angels bring them out of their hiding place and gather others, who have been saved during the last half of the Tribulation (Revelation 21:24).

Who is "the elect" referred to in Matthew 24:31 who come **from one end of heaven to the other?** The righteous redeemed who have gone to heaven either by physical death or by the catching up of the Body of Christ just before the beginning of the Tribulation and at Mid-Tribulation (Revelation 7:9-17).

The Elects Come Together!

Matthew 24:31 could just as easily read:

And Jesus, God's *Elect*, will send His *elect* angels to gather together His *elect* of Israel and others from all corners of the earth. Then the *elect* from one end of heaven to the other will join them as they come back from heaven to reign on the earth with the other three *elects* for a thousand years.

When studying the Scriptures and encountering the word *elect*, it then becomes necessary to allow the Scriptures to identify which elect is involved. In Matthew 24:31 all the *elects* are together. How absolutely glorious!

Do not look for the Rapture of the Church at the end of the Tribulation. That is when the Church returns from heaven to earth to reign for a thousand years. The Church will have been in heaven for seven years of worship, attending the Wedding of the Lamb and the Marriage Supper, and preparing for return with Jesus to earth (Zechariah 14:5; Revelation 17:14; 19:14).

"The Bridegroom Cometh!"

The Word of God says in First Thessalonians:

The Lord Himself will descend from heaven with a shout...and with the trumpet of God....

1 Thessalonians 4:16

In Revelation, chapter 4, we find an experience of the apostle John which parallels the Rapture of the Church. He heard a Voice that sounded like a trumpet, and he was taken in the spirit to heaven. With that "shout" John heard these words: **Come up here** (Revelation 4:1). I believe that a call like "Come up here" indicates the person being called is going to change locations.

I believe we are hearing a cry today: **Behold, the bridegroom cometh** (Matthew 25:6). Remember, when Jesus told this parable, that cry went out before the bridegroom came.

The Bride of Christ

Throughout generations, it has been generally accepted and taught that the Church is the Bride of Christ. Is this teaching true, or is it a major tradition without biblical support?

I ask in good faith that, before reaching your conclusion, you examine all the associated biblical references thoroughly, allowing the Scripture to speak for itself. This I have done, and I am satisfied.

Then one of the seven angels who had the seven bowls filled with the seven last plagues came to me and talked with me, saying, "Come, I will show you the bride, the Lamb's wife."

Revelation 21:9

There can be no argument as to the present identity of the Church. According to the apostle Paul, the Church is the Body of Christ, of which He is the Head

(See Colossians 1:18; Romans 12:5; Ephesians 1:22,23; 4:11-16).

Keep in mind that the terms *Church* and *Body of Christ* are interchangeable throughout Scripture. Also remember that although Jesus laid the foundation for the Church (Romans 15:20; 1 Corinthians 3:10-12) and is the Foundation as well as the Chief Cornerstone (Ephesians 2:20), it was the apostle Paul to whom the revelation of the Church was given. Paul clearly establishes himself as **the apostle of the Gentiles** (Romans 11:13).

I have learned through this study the difference between *identity* and *relationship*. Too often, believers have confused the two. When someone has a wrong identity, it is not likely he or she will develop a proper relationship with Jesus.

For as long as I can remember, it has been said that the Church is the Bride of Christ. This teaching has been based on the following Scripture references: Matthew 25:1-13, John 3:29 and Ephesians 5:24-30. Notice that not one of the above references identifies the Church as the Bride of Christ. As a matter of fact, there is not one verse of Scripture which says the Church is the Bride.

What then must we conclude? Apparently the Church has been given an identity that is incorrect.

This identity is based on assumption or what one may call a "type" or "shadow." It is true that there are many types and shadows in the Scriptures from which we receive insight into a truth. However, doctrine cannot be established on types and shadows.

The teaching that the Church is the Bride of Christ has become a doctrine within the Body of Christ without strong or clear support.

This teaching has been around for so many years that it has become traditional. Once a tradition has been established, it is difficult to remove. In fact, people will fight over their traditions. It is certainly reasonable that we would have extreme difficulty in questioning this traditional doctrine. How could so many men and women of God teach a tradition and overlook the soundness of the Word?

Perhaps an interpretation of Isaiah 54:5 has clouded our thinking. It says, **For your Maker is your husband**. There can be no mistake that God is the husband of the people of Israel as is so declared within that chapter. One could conclude that since God is married to Israel, then Jesus would take the Church as His Bride.

However, allow me to remind you that we are wrestling with identity versus relationship for the Church.

After serious study of all the Scriptures which seem to give the Church a "Bride identity," I discovered that all those references were teaching us relationship, not identity.

In Matthew 25, had the foolish virgins maintained a right relationship with the Bridegroom, they would not have been excluded from the marriage chamber. No one questions Jesus being the Bridegroom, but I must question that the virgins, wise or foolish, were to be the Bride. In the truest sense, they were friends of the Bridegroom. Some had maintained an up-to-date relationship with Him, while the others had not.

Consider John 3:29 in which John the Baptist, speaking of Jesus, makes a profound statement: **He who has the bride is the bridegroom**. Apparently there were people who thought John the Baptist to be the Christ. Why would anyone think that?

Remember, John was the first direct voice from God to the Israelites after the ministry of Malachi more than 400 years before. During that period, the people had the writings of Moses and the prophets with which to direct themselves. However, the priesthood was virtually backslidden, and idolatry was an everyday form of religion. Few of the people remained true to God.

Among the faithful were the priest Zacharias and his wife Elizabeth (Luke 1:5-25). Zacharias and Elizabeth were quite old when their son, John, was born. Among the youth who still loved and worshiped God, there were Mary and Joseph (Luke 1:26-38; Matthew 1:18-25).

Now back to John's statement. Notice he said, **He (Jesus) who *has* the bride is the bridegroom**. The word *has* is a present, passive participle indicating immediate possession. The remainder of John's statement recognizes the friends of the Bridegroom as those who stand with Him, hear Him and rejoice. When researching New Testament Church identity, one will find that those who stand, hear and rejoice are identified as the Church.

In Ephesians 5:24-30, carefully notice that these verses are describing the relationship between husband and wife, and do not lend themselves to one's identity. These Scriptures relate the Church to the Body of Christ, therefore making the Church a definite part of Jesus, the Bridegroom.

The identity of the Church as the Bride of Christ often prevents one from ever developing a strong, loving relationship with Jesus.

Throughout his epistles, the apostle Paul not only identifies the Church as the Body of Christ of which Christ is the Head, but he tells us we wear armor. (See Ephesians 6:10-17.) In Second Corinthians 10:4 he instructs us to use those weapons that are **mighty in God for pulling down strongholds**. Then he speaks, by the Holy Spirit, to Timothy and identifies him as **a good soldier of Jesus Christ** (2 Timothy 2:3).

We in the Body of Christ are involved in spiritual warfare. Armor and weapons are necessary and vital to every believer, along with the proper instructions as to how we are to wear and use that which God has supplied.

Revelation 19:14 further identifies us as an army, the same company called **saints** in Zechariah 14:5. Notice how in both places we are returning to the earth from heaven. We go up to heaven as victorious soldiers and return to earth with the same identity.

What more need I write? It is most evident that we, the Church, are not the Bride, but rather God's army in the world.

Someone has suggested that although we are presently believing soldiers, who are wearing armor and using weapons, we might become the Bride once we are taken up to heaven. My conclusion is based on Revelation 19:14 which shows the Church returning as the army of our Lord Jesus, not as His Bride.

Allow me to strongly urge every believer to recognize our identity as the Body of Christ and then work toward developing a wonderful relationship with Jesus.

Since it is biblically evident that the Church is not the Bride, then who is? For this information, one has to go to the book of Revelation, chapters 19 and 21.

Revelation 19:7 reads: **Let *us* be glad and rejoice and give Him glory, for the marriage of the Lamb has come, and His wife has made herself ready**. The opening verses set the location for the scene and the multitude present. Verse 7 addresses that multitude, making it clear that the Bride and the multitude are not one and the same. Notice also that the Bride, or the Lamb's Wife, is adorned with **fine linen**...the righteous acts of the **saints** (vs 8).

Let's remain with the book of Revelation and proceed to chapter 21. Begin carefully to read verse 1 and continue through verse 11. John, by the Holy Spirit, simply declares the city, New Jerusalem, to be the Lamb's Wife, or Bride, according to Revelation 21:2,9,10.

As you continue the study of chapters 21 and 22, you realize the New Jerusalem is no ordinary city. It cannot be compared with any city built by men.

We are programmed to think of a city as something like New York, Chicago, Los Angeles, Houston or the city of our *natural* birth. However, the New Jerusalem is the city associated with our *new* birth. It is supernatural and unlike any natural, existing city.

One may reason, *How can a city be the Bride of Christ?* The simplest answer is: this is the revelation the Holy Spirit gave to John. By faith, we must accept the revelation. Remember, **we walk by faith, not by sight** (2 Corinthians 5:7).

One may say, *I don't understand and I need understanding.* Again, I remind all of us that we are saved by grace through faith (Ephesians 2:8), and no one can explain the new birth any better than the Scriptures. We live by faith; and with the faith God has given us, we believe the written Word.

If one is not careful, it would be easy to take a "Thomas position" in relation to the New Jerusalem as the Bride of Christ. Thomas' position was: "I can't believe until I have understanding through my natural senses" (John 20:25).

Do not confuse the *identity* of the Church, which is the Body of Christ, with the *relationship* we must develop. Both are made very clear in the Scriptures.

It is possible this teaching about the identity of the Bride crosses swords with your traditional position. If so, only you can decide whether you will stay with tradition or allow the Word of God to speak for itself.

For the present, let us put on the whole armor of God, take up the mighty weapons of God as good soldiers, and by faith carry out our assignment as the army and Body of Christ in this present world.

Whether you agree or disagree with the identity of the Bride of Christ will not affect your salvation, but it could affect your Christian lifestyle.

I have met multitudes of Christians who seldom wear armor or use God's weapons. Rarely do they attack Satan or do his kingdom any harm. In fact, Satan beats, cheats and robs them on a regular basis. The reason for the above condition is the lack of true identity and failure to develop a proper relationship with Jesus.

One last thought provoking question: *If the Church is the Bride of Christ, as is often taught, why was John shown something different?* I rest my case!

Be Ready!

You can be a wise virgin who is ready to go into the marriage chamber of Matthew 25, or you can be a foolish virgin who misses the Rapture when Jesus shouts, Come up here! Either you are ready, or you are not. The choice is yours.

I urge you: get ready now to be caught away in the Rapture with Jesus, and stay ready daily. One maintains a ready condition by walking with the Lord every day (Genesis 5:22; Hebrews 11:5,6).

---

[1] *Webster's New World Dictionary*, 2d College ed., s.v. "rapture."
[2] Ibid., s.v. "ecstasy."

Chapter 11
A More Sure Word of Prophecy

Jesus is coming soon!

This declaration should become part of *every* Christian's vocabulary.

As I was growing up in church, I was impacted by this thought: *Jesus is coming soon!* People were always saying it. They sang about it, praised God for it and preached it often. Heaven was mixed with this thought. Many had heaven on their minds.

But time went by. I grew into adolescence — He didn't come.

I grew into my teenage years — He didn't come.

I grew into young manhood — He still hadn't come.

Over sixty years have come and gone since I first was really affected by the statement: *Jesus is coming soon!*

One may point out, "That's a long time to believe Jesus is coming soon and the event not take place."

True, but you and I are that much closer to His return.

Through the years in church, I did not have the prophecies being fulfilled to set the stage for His appearing.

113

But I have them now. Hallelujah!

Believers need to be conducting their lives in such a way that they are ready when He comes. Not hoping to be ready. Not thinking, *Oh, one of these days I'll be ready, but I'm just too busy now.*

If you are only hoping you are ready, then you are not ready.

If you are saying, "Well, I think maybe I'm ready," then you are not ready.

If there is sin in your life, you are not ready.

If you are lukewarm like those of the Laodicean church, you are not ready (See Revelation 3:15,16).

If you are like the foolish virgins in Matthew 25, you are not ready.

So you have a choice: you can get yourself ready for the events that are going to come, or you can keep fooling around and wait too long.

The Word declares to be carnally minded is death but to be spiritually minded is life (Romans 8:6). In years past, some in the Church were so heavenly minded they were no earthly good. These days in many churches people are so earthly minded they are of no spiritual benefit. A change is in order. Both our vocabulary and our thoughts must begin to reflect the Scriptures we profess to believe.

Fables vs. the Truth

Let us examine several verses in Second Peter, chapter 1. The apostle Peter declared:

For we did not followed cunningly devised fables when we made known to you the power and coming of our Lord Jesus Christ, but were eyewitnesses of His majesty.
2 Peter 1:16

In other words, Peter was saying, "We have shared with you Jesus Christ because we were eyewitnesses of what He did and hearers of what He taught."

Peter also wrote:

For He received from God the Father honor and glory when such a voice came to Him from the Excellent Glory: "This is My beloved Son, in whom I am well pleased."

And we heard this voice which came from heaven when we were with Him on the holy mountain.

2 Peter 1:17,18

What was this **holy mountain** to which Peter refers? The mount of transfiguration.

Peter states: "We [Peter, James, John] were with Jesus on the mount of transfiguration. We saw Him in His glory and heard the Father say, 'This is My beloved Son in Whom I am well pleased.'" Remember, that was the same occasion in which Moses and Elijah came and stood beside Jesus Christ on the mount (Matthew 17:1-8).

Prophetic Word Made More Sure

Peter continues:

And so we have the prophetic word confirmed [more sure KJV]....

2 Peter 1:19

How can the prophetic Word of God become more sure? Through its literal fulfillment.

There are many prophecies in the Scriptures which have already been fulfilled; so many, in fact, that we can be absolutely certain about the authority of God's Word.

What does prophetic fulfillment do for the Scriptures as a whole? It convinces us that the Word has proceeded from God. We become sure of the Word's divine inspiration and its accuracy.

Many biblical prophecies are in the process of fulfillment today. To detail them requires an additional book.

Prophecy Is Like Light Shining in the Dark

What did Peter say?

And so we have the prophetic word confirmed, [more sure KJV] which you do well to heed as a light that shines in a dark place.... 2 Peter 1:19

No wonder the Devil doesn't want you enjoying God's prophetic Word. It is a brilliant light for the dark world.

God's word of prophecy is like a light that shines in a dark place. Psalm 119:105 says, **Your word is a lamp to my feet and a light to my path.**

When Israel became a nation on May 15, 1948, a major prophetic event had begun to be fulfilled. When that occurred, the Body of Christ should have exploded with excitement. The truth of the matter is, very few members of His Body reacted in that way. Why? Because Satan had either blinded them to the Truth or so kept them out of the prophecies that they were not aware of what had happened.

Many of God's people missed it. We can no longer afford to be uninformed when it comes to the prophecies of Scripture.

God's Prophecies Are Settled in Heaven

The statement of Peter continues to demand our attention:

> **...you do well to heed as a light that shines in a dark place, until the day dawns and the morning star rises in your hearts;**
>
> **knowing this first, that no prophecy of Scripture is of any private interpretation.**
>
> **2 Peter 1:19,20**

I pointed out earlier the office of the prophet. Their prophecies in the Old Testament have a higher priority than the office of the prophet in the New Testament.

How do we know that? Because the prophecies in the written Word of God are already settled in heaven. They do not need to be examined or proved. But the prophecies of today's prophet or one operating in the gift of prophecy, as the apostle Paul teaches, must be judged and proved before we do anything with them. (Psalm 119:89; 1 Corinthians 2:15; 1 John 4:1).

The Season of His Appearing

In light of all that is happening in our world today, we are aware of the fulfillment of many biblical prophecies. The season in which Jesus is to appear has dawned. This revelation must be permitted to cause a change for greater spiritual life in every believer.

We must allow the light of God's Word to drive out all darkness.

The Church must rid itself of besetting sins and lay aside all the weights and hindering cares of this life (Hebrews 12:1).

Without question, we are living in the last days. We are in the Friday of those days. It is the time of the end.

Prophecies of the Scriptures are escalating, and Jesus is coming soon!

The apostle Paul writes in Romans 10:13:

For "whoever calls on the name of the Lord shall be saved."

Why not do that now if you have not already done so? A simple statement in which you recognize Jesus as God's Son and invite Him to become your Savior will change your life.

According to Romans 10:9,10:

...if you confess with your mouth the Lord Jesus and believe in your heart that God has raised Him from the dead, you will be saved.

For with the heart one believes to righteousness, and with the mouth confession is made to salvation.

Appendix
12
Biblical Rules of Interpretation

The study of the Scriptures reveals several built-in rules that assist us both with proper interpretation and rightly dividing the Word of Truth.

The first rule to consider is the rule of double reference.

It becomes evident from the study of the Old Testament that there are many truths and instructions which also apply to the Church. Let us not forget that, although Jesus delivered us from the curse of the Law, He did not do away with the righteousness of the Law. Therefore, when one of the Old Testament writers sets forth righteous instructions, it is as much for us as it was for the people of Israel. Also, when God pronounced blessings, they are equally ours through Jesus Christ (Galatians 3:13,14). Since God is not a respecter of persons, He would not work miracles for Israel and not do the same for us.

We are also instructed to recognize the examples within the Old Testament of both the successes and failures of Israel, thereby learning and benefiting from their record (1 Corinthians 10:11).

Another rule of interpretation covers the use of the word *sea*. There are numerous times in which it refers to an existing body of water. When that is not the case, it will be identifying a mass of humanity — a sea of people.

When reading the Scripture and the word *sea* appears, examine the entire passage of Scripture sufficiently to determine whether it is indeed identifying a body of water or referring to masses of people.

The book of Revelation provides us some good examples. One is found in chapter 17 in which the harlot is described as sitting upon many waters. The fifteenth verse of that chapter clearly describes the many waters as peoples, multitudes and nations.

First Samuel 13:5 provides us another excellent example of this rule; and there are a number of others.

A similar rule covers the use of the word *mountain*. When reading Scripture in which the word *mountain* is used, if an existing mountain of rock is not identified by name or geographical location, then it is identifying a kingdom. The words *mountain* and *kingdom* become interchangeable.

An excellent example is found in Daniel, chapter 2, verses 34,35,44. You will notice in verse 35 the word *mountain* is used, while in verse 44 the word *kingdom* is used, both identifying the same majestic act of the Almighty.

These simple rules will often enable you to have good understanding of the scriptural account.

Appendix
13

How Important Are the Prophecies of the Scriptures?

It is apparent that God thought His prophecy to be of utmost importance. Why so?

Consider these facts:

• The Old Testament begins with a prophecy and has within itself sixteen books dedicated to the subject. God closes the Old Testament with the prophetic book of Malachi.

• The New Testament begins with an Old Testament prophecy being fulfilled: the birth of Jesus. It contains the prophetic words of Jesus and writings of Paul, Peter, and John in his book of Revelation, which closes the Testament.

The first prophetic utterance is found in Genesis 3:15. Following Satan's (or the Serpent's) deception of Eve, God prophesied directly to him (paraphrasing): "Because of what you have done, I will put hatred between you and the Seed of the woman." Here's the prophecy: "The Seed of the woman will bruise your head."

Satan quickly caused trouble in the family. He gained influential control of Cain and, through him, destroyed Abel. He surely gloated over his success, thinking, *I can disarm or short-circuit God's prophecy.*

However, after Adam and Eve were removed from the Garden, Seth was born. The Scripture is clear: Adam and Eve raised Seth to know God and walk uprightly before Him (Genesis 4:25,26). Seth continued the family tree, producing a righteous lineage from whom would come the Seed destined to permanently bruise Satan's head: JESUS.

Two important truths spring from the Scriptures:

1. Adam and Eve were not totally depraved and cut off from God. True, they lost their estate in the Garden, but God maintained a relationship with them for the sake of His Word.

2. Since Jesus is referred to as **the last Adam** (1 Corinthians 15:45), we have insight as to why Adam ate of the forbidden fruit, although he was not deceived. He loved Eve so much he gave himself for her; he could not envision himself separated from her. In the first Adam, we see a type of the last Adam, Jesus, Who knowing no sin became sin **that we might become the righteousness of God in Him** (2 Corinthians 5:21). So, the first Adam with his human nature was also a type of Christ, because of love.

An interesting story line develops throughout the Old Testament. It portrays Satan constantly struggling to cut off the Seed of the woman. He worked overtime in his attempt to destroy Israel and end God's plan. Thank God he failed and Jesus came, bruising his head just as God had prophesied 4,000 years before.

Notice God, with no concern for Satan, caused him untold insecurity and anguish. Daily, Satan had to contend with the fact that Someone was on the way to inflict total defeat upon him.

What can we conclude concerning Satan, our adversary? He has a proven track record as an absolute failure!

No wonder Paul instructs, "Give no place to the devil" (Ephesians 4:27). When one gives himself over to satanic influence, he has allowed the "master failure" to take control. *The end result is **always** failure.*

Satan has a serious hatred for the prophecies of the Scripture. He discovered that when God prophesies, it *always* comes to pass. Satan has not ceased to oppose the prophetic writings in God's Word. He has shrouded them with a veil of confusion, causing many ministers and laymen to either ignore or bypass the sixteen Old Testament prophetic books and the book of Revelation.

Through the years I have heard learned men of God reveal their personal attitude toward these majestic books.

Some have declared, "The prophecies of the Scripture tend to confuse the reader." If this were true, God lied when He said He was not the author of confusion (1 Corinthians 14:33).

It has also been stated: "The prophetic books, including Revelation, are not as important to daily Christian living as are the other forty-nine books of the Bible." Were such a statement true, the apostle Paul did not know the truth when he wrote: **All scripture is given by inspiration of God, and is profitable for doctrine, for reproof, for correction, for instruction in righteousness, that the man** [or woman] **of God may be complete, thoroughly equipped for every good work** (2 Timothy 3:16,17).

The Church — you and I — must divorce itself from the traditions of men. God will not accept our cop-outs on His Word. Cop-outs are always based upon either ignorance of the subject, laziness, or established traditional thinking.

The prophetic books were given by the same Holy Spirit that gave us Genesis, Psalms, Proverbs, the Gospels, Acts and all the other marvelously wonderful books. God did not insert or add the seventeen prophetic books so He could say, "Look how thick My Book is!" The books of prophecy and the many other prophetic statements are not there for filler! They relate to John 3:16 — God's love. All believers must become possessors of truth or be subject to deception by the one who hates the prophecies of the Scripture.

Can one benefit from the books of prophecy? Yes, emphatically!

When read and studied without fear, these books definitely edify. They contain a beautiful and interesting story of God's relationship with a people of His choosing. One learns the historical background of the natural seed of Abraham, the children of Israel. An additional and very important benefit is provided when one discovers the fulfillment of ancient prophecies. Actually a masterful performance of God keeping His Word is clearly evident.

One cannot gain such edification, knowledge and firsthand awareness of God's performance without it having a profound and wholesome effect on his faith.

Remember, **faith comes by hearing, and hearing by the word of God** (Romans 10:17). I strongly recommend you read the Scripture aloud to yourself.

Other books by Hilton Sutton Th.D.

The Antichrist
The Next Ressurection…you may never die
Revelation Revealed
The Revelation Teaching Syllabus
The United States in Prophecy
Deacons

For More infomation
or to place an order please contact us:

Hilton Sutton World Ministries
PO Box 1259
New Caney, TX 77357
U.S.A.
(281) 689-1260
FAX: (281) 689-1265
www.hilton-sutton.org
hsm@hilton-sutton.org

About the Author

Dr. Hilton Sutton is one of the world's foremost authorities on the prophetic scriptures, including the Book of Revelation. He is in great demand as a speaker for churches, Bible colleges, national and international conventions, and for radio and television audiences in the United States, Canada, and around the world. He teaches Bible Prophecy without doom and gloom or speculation, in an edifying way that inspires victory, joy, peace, and hope. His exciting Bible based positive messages have brought many thousands to salvation and set believers free from unscriptural fear of the future.

Presently Hilton is Chairman of the Board of Hilton Sutton World Ministries, with offices in Roman Forest, Texas and London, Ontario, Canada. He is a member of the Executive Board of World Ministry Fellowship of Plano, Texas, and was a founding trustee of the International Charismatic Bible Ministries of Tulsa, Oklahoma. He is also an active member of the International Convention of Faith Ministries of Arlington, Texas and F.C.F. of Tulsa, Oklahoma.

He has personally addressed the Joint Chiefs of Staff of the United States Military, the Israeli Knesset and the Israeli Foreign Ministry. He is acquainted with past Israeli Prime Minister Benjamin Netanyahu, and his personal friends include past Israeli Prime Ministers Shimon Peres, Yitzak Shamir, and the late Yitzak Rabin and Menachem Begin.

His books, audio, and video tapes have blessed and edified tens of thousands of people in many nations. Hilton's twelve-hour study of the Book of Revelation available on audio or video tape with accompanying syllabus, makes this vitally important book a pleasure to study and simple to understand. It is offered as a course for certificate credit at Oral Roberts University, and also may be taken by correspondence.

Dr. Sutton has authored fifteen books, including a verse-by-verse study of the Book of Revelation entitled "Revelation Revealed,"New titles include "The Antichrist," Discovering Ancient Prophecies," and "The Next Resurrection." His ministry produces a video of the prophecies of the scripture and review of current world events entitled "Insight To The Future." This 45 to 50 minute program is designed for churches to share with their congregations and is also available to individual subscribers. Hilton's over fifty three years of studying and preaching the prophecies of the Scripture qualify him as the senior prophetic teacher of our day.